Marketing For Writers Who Hate Marketing: The No-Stress Way to Sell Books Without Losing Your Mind

MARKETING FOR WRITERS WHO HATE MARKETING

The No-Stress Way to Sell Books Without Losing Your Mind

James Scott Bell

Compendium Press

Compendium Press
P.O. Box 705
Woodland Hills, CA 91365

ISBN 10: 0-910355-35-5
ISBN 13: 978-0-910355-35-3

Table of Contents

1

What, You Worry?

Something may be sucking the joy out of your creative spirit. It may be stomping all over your writing happiness. Heck, it may even have you thinking about quitting.

You're a writer who just wants to write. You want to string words together and weave a dream. You love that glorious synchronicity between author and reader, when someone says those glorious words, "I couldn't put it down!"

You live for the blast of being a writer.

What you don't live for is marketing.

Oh, you accept it. You accept it the way you do your screwball uncle who shows up at Thanksgiving dinner and won't stop talking about the global conspiracy to inject baby seals with steroids that will turn them into killer sharks, which will be the cause of a *real* Sharknado, thank you very much.

Yes, you accept him and feed him turkey because, well, he comes with the family territory.

But all you really want to do is get up from the table, go take a nap, find a room where you can be alone, and get back to writing.

7

Maybe it's that marketing intimidates you. You look around and see writers who are marketing machines. They're like little terminators who never stop coming at you. You can't escape them. They're on Twitter and Facebook and Google+ and Goodreads and Instagram and Pinterestevery day!—not to mention their blogs. In their spare time they host podcasts and add content to their own YouTube channels.

Oh yes, and they write a lot of books and make a ton of money and you think, *Man! I can't possibly do even half that much! I'm destined to be a dreg in the bottom of the Amazon rankings, so what's the point in going on? Maybe Wal-Mart needs another greeter. Or perhaps I can apply to be a price checker at the 99¢ store.*

If that's you, writer friend, I'm here to tell you to take heart. You don't have to love marketing, nor do you have to get sucked into its vortex in order to be good at it.

You can be an effective marketer without it:

- taking away from your creativity
- taking away from the quality of your writing
- taking away from the parts of your life that also matter, like friends and family
- causing you stress
- making you envious of others
- turning you into a bitter complainer who no one wants to be around

I wrote this book after hearing from several of my writing colleagues over the last few years. These are all writers who have been (and some who still are) part of what's called traditional publishing. They were given contracts by publishing houses and happily went about building a career.

As the digital boom took off, publishers started pushing their writers to do more marketing on social media. For a number of my friends this was an added stressor they didn't want or need.

Then, post 2007 and the introduction of the Kindle, self-publishing became a real and potentially lucrative option for writers who know their craft. A number of my friends began sticking toes in the indie waters. I was waist deep, and some asked me if they should venture out further.

"The water's fine," I said.

As time went on, however, I started hearing things like:

I wish I could just write!

Marketing is taking up too much of my time!

I don't know what works!

I keep trying things, and I'm frustrated!

Writing isn't fun anymore!

I finally decided I had to write this book. My primary goal is to help you prioritize your marketing so you can concentrate on the handful of tools that are most effective, and eliminate the worry that you're never doing enough.

And it begins with the best news of all: the single most important marketing tool, by far, is one you already love!

2
The Single Most Important Marketing Tool

That's right.

The most important marketing tool you will ever wield is one you already love.

And it's a tool you can sharpen each day without taking a single thing away from your writing.

Because *it is* your writing.

Your books, your stories, the way you connect with readers. By far and away, this is the golden key to selling your work.

As super-agent Donald Maass says, "The best marketing comes between the covers of the book."

On the other hand—and this is one gigantic hand—if your book is not quality, you've lost that book buyer, probably for good. You can have a razzle-dazzle marketing plan. You can pay for costly advertising. You can do social media out the wazoo (and you know how painful that can be!). But all of that only gets you an introduction. Your book must convert the intro into a lasting relationship.

A survey commissioned by digital aggregator Smashwords some years ago asked how e-book buyers found the titles they purchased. The results were posted on their blog on September 24, 2011.

- The most-selected answer was "Recommendations from fellow readers on online message forums, blogs and message boards," with 29% of respondents choosing this.
- The second most common answer was, "I look first for my favorite authors," coming in at 18%.
- Retailer recommendations (e.g., "Also bought") was 5%.
- Personal recommendation from a friend or family member was 4%.
- Reviews from trusted sources, 3%.
- Scanning the bestseller list, 3%.

Add that up, and you get a whopping 62% that relates to some form of word-of-mouth, including the readers' own mouths in the case of favorite authors!

Word-of-mouth operates completely apart from what we think of as marketing. It's not something you can manufacture or buy. It's organic and flows out of the books and stories you write.

The next biggest segment of discovery in that survey was browsing, whether it was online or at a brick-and-mortar store.

Among browsers, 7% said they looked at covers, and if one "grabbed" them, they investigated further.

Another 4% said they would "sample anything."

Since the most important marketing tool is the quality of your books, becoming the best writer you can be is job #1. This is where the majority of your time should be spent.

Productivity as a writer is also a marketing tool. The more you write, with quality, the more you grow a "long tail" that has renewed life with each new book.

Yes, you'll have some work to do when it comes to covers, book description copy and other "metadata" (like keywords and categories).

And we'll talk about the all-important email list.

But once you get a handle on these things, everything else in the marketing spectrum fades in comparison.

Do a few things well, not everything with mediocrity.

Since quality writing is paramount, I encourage you to put in place a method of constant and never-ending improvement.

A Writing Improvement Plan

In Japan, after World War II, the concept of *kaizen* was introduced into their industrial culture. It resulted in a huge boom in technology and manufacturing that rebuilt Japan and made her prosperous.

It's a simple idea. It means ongoing quality, and systems set up to test quality all the time. And, every day, striving to do something better.

Why should a writer do any less?

You are responsible for designing your own writing improvement program. One that never ends.

But most writers don't think in a *kaizen* type of manner. We are artists, after all! We want to frolic in the tulip fields of the imagination! We don't want to get weighed down with things like, yikes, strategic planning! We could have gone to engineering school if we wanted to do that kind of thing.

Really, it's not that difficult.

If you're a fiction writer, you can break down your craft into seven critical success areas:

1. Plot
2. Structure
3. Characters

4. Scenes
5. Dialogue
6. Voice
7. Theme

You can design an ongoing self-study program that takes you through each of these areas, as many times as you want.

What if you set a goal to improve in each area, by 10%, every year? (That 10% is an arbitrary figure, of course. It's more of a feeling you get, that you've upped your game. It doesn't have to be a lot. Just 10% a year.)

Your writing improvement would be steady, which in turn improves your books, which in turn improves your word-of-mouth, which is the number one tool of marketing!

Win-win-win.

How do you design self-study?

1. Pick an area.

2. Make a list of some novels you read that did particularly well in this area. For plot you might select a Dean Koontz. For dialogue, an Elmore Leonard. For characters, Jodi Picoult. The list is endless, and you know the books you've liked. Re-read those books and take notes on what you observe the author does well.

3. Select good craft books to study in the area of your concentration. In the back of this book you will find a list of my own resources for writing improvement. There are many other excellent teachers and resources available to you by searching them out.

4. Do some practice writing in the area. Sample scenes where you're trying out the techniques you learn.

5. Get feedback. You can get this from trusted friends, critique partners or groups, and even on occasion a paid critique, as from the Writer's Digest 2nd Draft service.

If you're writing nonfiction, you also need a continuing improvement program. Obviously, continue to read and study and experiment with your area of interest.

1. Keep improving your ability to write clearly. A book that should be on every writer's shelf, and periodically perused, is William Zinsser's *On Writing Well*.

2. Study books on the art and craft of nonfiction. I'll give you one right now: *Writers Inc.* by Patrick Sebranek, Dave Kemper, and Verne Meyer. This book is designed to be a text for high schoolers, but writers of any age will find it highly instructive. It's a tad pricey, but if you were to pay for a course on writing, you'd spend a lot more. You can use this book as a study program (by going through it chapter by chapter), or as handy reference guide.

3. Get serious about grammar. Learn to avoid the obvious mistakes (there will be enough subtle mistakes to go around). While many writers still recommend the venerable *Elements of Style* by Strunk & White, my favorite desk reference is *Write Right!* by Jan Venolia.

4. Find a good freelance editor who knows the rules of grammar. Such editors are getting harder to come by, because they're not being trained much anymore. From time to time give this editor some dough to go over your work.

5. Improve your vocabulary. The classic work on this is *Word Power Made Easy* by Norman Lewis.

Choosing What to Write

If you are looking at writing as a true vocation, part of your long-term marketing will involve choosing what to write.

There are some writers who want to write whatever they want to write, and that's fine.

Other writers try to figure out what sells best, what's hot, and then write that kind of thing. That's okay, too. We live in a free enterprise system.

My philosophy as a writer (who wanted to make a living as a writer) was to look for that sweet spot where my passion met commercial viability. In my mind was this diagram:

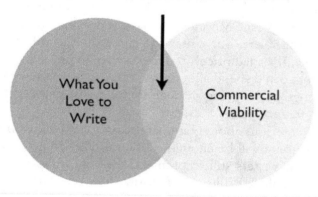

The Successful Book

What You Love to Write

Commercial Viability

This applies to both fiction and nonfiction. You'll always write better what you're most interested in.

Before I was a traditionally published fiction author, I was very much influenced by the be-bop stylings of Mr. Jack Kerouac. He was launched by his famous book *On the Road,* which read like cool jazz. Kerouac wrote a whole lot of books after that, most of which we would call experimental in style. Which meant they did not sell.

I thought that writing from the gut like Kerouac was the key to the whole matter. But when I didn't sell anything, nor garner any interest, I decided I had to learn something about both craft and market.

Eventually, it hit me with a great, big *DUH.*

I was a practicing lawyer. Legal thrillers were hot.

Also, I liked thrillers as a genre. That's mostly what I read with my discretionary time.

So, dope (I told myself), why don't you write a legal thriller?

That's exactly what I did, and it led to a multi-book contract with a publishing house, and launched my career.

In this way I wrote what I loved and also what had a chance to sell.

So ask yourself some questions:

1. What kind of fiction do you like to read?

2. What kind of story do you like to write?

3. How would you describe the genre of your work-in-progress?

4. How popular is that genre in the marketplace?

5. Can you adjust? Is there another genre you enjoy that might gain better traction?

6. If you really love what you're writing, how can you tweak it to gain more marketability? For example, readers generally prefer fiction that makes them feel good at the end. They also favor fiction with characters they can root for.

Also, consider writing a series. Each book in the series works to help sell the others. The key, of course, is to create a unique, compelling, unforgettable series character. Like Harry Bosch (Michael Connelly) or Stephanie Plum (Janet Evanovich). In 1968 a 41-year-old ex-Navy man named Don Pendleton decided to try his hand at writing an action novel. *The Executioner: War Against the Mafia* came out in 1968. It featured a Vietnam vet named Mack Bolan who takes his military skills to the streets against the Cosa Nostra. Pendleton wrote 36 books in the series before licensing the rights to a publishing house (which in turn hired ghostwriters). The series has sold over 200 million copies.

So yeah, a series can be a great idea.

Assess your preference every six months or so. Nothing is static in the world. The book marketplace is a roiling sea. My favorite metaphor of the successful author is … a cork! Ride the waves. Keep your head above water.

All of the above is for the improvement of your most important asset, your greatest marketing tool—your books themselves. By studying your craft you are automatically, simultaneously, and without further effort working on your marketing.

That is what I call good news indeed.

3
The All-Important First Impression

They say the first seven seconds you interact with a person forms their first impression. And it's tough to change it after that.

Thus, if you enter a business meeting dressed like a slob, hair unkempt and smelling like last night's beer party, your chances of success are diminished accordingly.

But what if you enter the room wearing a sharp, uncreased suit, your hair perfect, and, if you're a man, you're freshly shaved, unless you can rock a beard without looking like a guy who writes manifestos in the wilderness.

If you're a woman, you don't have a tag sticking up in the back of your collar or crumbs from your morning bagel on your blouse.

Your handshake is firm, but not crushing.

And when you smile, no spinach on your teeth.

You can make a good first impression. It inspires momentary trust. It takes the initial burden off you.

It's the same with your book cover, which I would place as your second most important marketing tool, right after the book itself. Why? Because if potential readers are turned off by the cover, you may not move them to the cover copy (also known as the book description) or to the writing itself (your first few pages, also called the sample).

You're going to need a cover anyway, so make it a good one.

How?

By hiring someone to do it.

Do not try to do it yourself.

Okay, if you're really daring, have real artistic ability, and want to give it a try yourself, fine. But in 99 cases out of 100, a pro can do it better.

Yes, it's an upfront cost, but it will be a first impression forever. So it pays to make it a good one.

From Bland to Brand

Back in the "old days" (like, before August, 2010) branding was a key concept in the traditional publishing world. Still is, actually. That's because a publisher trying to make money with an author has to build a readership, and that's done over time, book by book. Readers who start becoming fans expect that new books by the author will be similar in tone and genre to the ones they've enjoyed.

Take a hypothetical author. He comes out with a terrific first novel, a thriller about a boy on the run from the law. A fan base starts to form and they eagerly await his next book. If that book were to be about a horticulture competition in Surrey, England, circa 1849, they would tend to be confused and frustrated. They might decide to skip the next book he writes because they're not sure what it contains.

So author and publisher come out with another thriller, this one about a family on the run from the FBI. Fans buy it and are happy. They start spreading the word to other thriller fans about this fellow. The growing base looks forward to the next thriller. Publisher is very happy about this, and signs up author for more books.

Now, if an author under this traditional system became overwhelmingly popular, like a King, Grisham, or Patterson, they earned the right to try, on occasion, something "off brand." King might write about a girl lost in the woods. Grisham about a painted house. Patterson about whatever the heck he wants—I have a feeling his parking tickets would sell a million copies.

But the traditional publishers will insist on getting "back on brand" with the next book, because that is the bread and butter for them, the guaranteed sales.

Branding in the days of print-only was partially determined by physical shelf space and seasonal purchases. An author could not come out with several different titles at roughly the same time. Bookstores wouldn't buy. And they'd be a bit confused. If our hypothetical thriller author did write that horticulture romance, *A Garden in My Heart*, would it be placed on the thriller shelf next to his other titles, where fans would look? Or on the romance shelf? Or with the gardening books?

But there are no such limitations in the digital world. All books are "shelved" cover out. Digitized books are given, via algorithm, space next to similar books. A reader can find new authors in a genre this way.

Simply put, if you are writing in a genre, make sure your covers look like books of that genre. Readers expect that. Don't make their search harder than it needs to be.

This is just common sense.

If you are planning to self-publish in a different genre, you brand that work not by your name but by your cover. You get a design that readers of that genre will respond to.

As an aside, in the "old days" a writer doing different genres usually employed a pseudonym. That was so they could easily be shelved in a different part of a store and would not throw off their loyal readers. Many times a writer would use a pen name because he or she was "slumming" in a genre neighborhood and didn't want that stigma attached to their official name. For example, the novelist Evan Hunter wrote contemporary, standalone fiction that he considered to be literary. But to make some much-needed dough, he started writing a series of police procedural mysteries under the name Ed McBain. I think Hunter was somewhat annoyed that McBain became the huge bestseller. He assuaged his annoyance by cashing all the royalty checks.

These days, unless a traditional publisher insists on it, there's no good reason to use a pseudonym. Using one name allows a bit of "cross-pollination" between genres. Some readers who like your thrillers may give your romances a shot.

Bottom line: Brand your book covers so readers have an inkling of what to expect inside, even if they do not read the cover copy.

And if you're writing a series, brand that particular series as well. In other words, if you have four cat-lover mysteries featuring the same lovable sleuth, each cover should use the same font and basic design ... and probably have a cat, too.

Again, common sense. You're making things easy for the browser and potential buyer.

So let's talk about the steps to take when getting a good cover.

How do you find good cover designers?

1. Get a recommendation from a writer whose covers you admire.

2. Find great looking covers on Amazon or in a bookstore. You'll often find the cover designer's name on the copyright page or the back cover. In any event, save the book images for

future reference. When you hire a designer, you can show the comps.

3. Search the internet for freelance book cover designers. Go to the website and check out the portfolio and client list. Joanna Penn, a well-known indie writer and blogger, has a page of cover designer names. Go to:

www.thecreativepenn.com/bookcoverdesign/

4. Check out 99designs.com. They offer design services that are reasonably priced.

How to work with a cover artist

1. Show a few examples of the kind of cover look you want.

2. Provide your cover copy (see next chapter).

3. Give the designer some preliminary suggestions of what you'd like the cover to look like. Image, of course. If you have a great tag line (again, next chapter), consider that for the cover as well.

4. Agree up front on the number of changes you can request.

5. Be sure to negotiate both an e-book and a print cover.

How much should you expect to pay?

As of this writing, a good cover can run you $200–$500. More if it is artistically intense (such as for an epic fantasy). For $299, 99designs will generate thirty covers from various designers for you to choose from.

What NOT to do with your cover

Unless you have had a string of bestselling books, do not put your name in large font across the top of your cover. Do not render your name in larger font than your title. You want people drawn to the title and the cover image, not to a name they are likely to be unfamiliar with.

What if I want to do short fiction or articles?

If you plan on publishing a lot of short fiction or nonfiction, cover design will be your biggest cost. But if you consider shorter works primarily as a way of enticing new readers to your work (see Chapter 12), this cost represents an investment. It's like a billboard. You want it to be visually pleasing and get the message across.

You have a couple of options regarding this cost.

First is good old negotiation. Ask if the designer will consider a price break on covers for stories or nonfiction shorts. Obviously, be willing to accept less of a time commitment on their part. But if they're professional, they will in most cases provide a professional-looking product.

A second option is to propose a template design for stories or articles in the same genre. You can ask the designer to create a basic look, which means your name and the title would stay in the same font and in the same location on each cover. The only tweak would be to the background. This might involve a different image or color scheme.

For my boxing stories featuring Irish Jimmy Gallagher, I designed a pulp-style template with the same background image, changing only the color and title.

4

Cover Copy That Sizzles and Sells

Yes, you're a writer who hates marketing. But you know that the ability to write copy that describes your books and entices readers to buy them is essential.

This is called copywriting. It is the art of the ad man, or ad woman. It is the skill of the salesperson. It is the practice of moving people to action by your words.

You will be writing copy to describe your books, and in emails to your fans that alert them to your offerings.

Good copy is clear, easy-to-read, persuasive. It uses short sentences and eschews words like *eschews*. A good rule of thumb is that you want your copy to be understandable to a seventh grader.

Let's apply this to the copy that describes your book, and your author bio.

Just a word on *metadata*. This word sometimes sends shivers up writers who love to write. It shouldn't. All it means is information *about* your book that is implanted in certain places. For example, when you're publishing through Kindle Direct Publishing, you are given a place for keyword search terms (we cover keywords later in this chapter). That's an example of metadata. Don't stress about it. We'll go over the most important aspects of metadata in a natural fashion as we move along.

Cover Copy

Cover copy—also called the book description—is the sizzle that gets browsers to cut a slice of steak. Studies have shown that book browsing in stores follows this pattern:

A cover catches your eye.

You pick it up and read the dust jacket copy or, in the case of a paperback, the back cover copy.

You look at the author bio.

You read the first few pages.

You look at the price of the book. If all the other factors have given you pleasure, your resistance at shelling out dough is overcome.

You buy the book.

You make the author happy.

The Value of Good Copy in the Writing Process

Being able to write good cover copy yourself is not just part of marketing. It helps you focus your writing, too. In fiction writing, we sometimes talk about the "pantser" (who likes to write without planning) and the "plotter" (who likes to outline or plan ahead).

With nonfiction, there are those who like to do extensive research and organization first, and those who like to wing it and discover their subject as they go along.

No matter what your preference, learning to craft a good description early on will save you a lot of grief down the line.

A Formula for Fiction

Here is a simple formula for fiction cover copy that works every time. Follow the formula strictly at first, then you can tweak it any way you like. The formula consists of three one-sentence paragraphs.

Sentence #1 is a character name, vocation, and opening situation.

Sentence #2 begins with *But when* and lays out the turning point in the story, the entry into the central conflict. (I call this the Doorway of No Return in my book *Plot & Structure*. Some call it the first "plot point" while others may use "inciting incident." What matters is that it has to be something that *pushes* the protagonist into the conflict of Act 2. Otherwise, there really is no story.)

Sentence #3 begins with *Now* and lays out what I call the "death stakes." (To have an optimal plot, death must be on the line. There are three types of death—physical, professional, psychological. Unless the stakes feel that way to your protagonist, the readers won't be fully engaged.)

Here is an example of how cover copy might be done for a novelization of the classic 1939 movie, *The Wizard of Oz* (apologies to L. Frank Baum):

> Dorothy Gale is a farm girl who dreams of getting out of Kansas to a land far, far away where she and her dog will be safe from the likes of town busybody, Miss Gulch.
>
> But when a twister hits the farm, Dorothy is transported to a land of strange creatures and at least one wicked witch who wants to kill her.
>
> Now, with the help of three unlikely friends, Dorothy must find a way to destroy a

wicked witch who wants her dead—and thus convince a great wizard to send her back home.

The nice thing about this formula is that it becomes what's called your "elevator pitch." That's what writers call an informal exchange with someone who wants to know what your book's about. As in an elevator, where you have only a couple of floors to give it to them.

These three sentences may work as is. Or you may want to add a bit to each paragraph, or play with the wording. It's up to you.

I advise writers to come up with this cover copy early in their writing process. It doesn't matter whether you like to plan out your novels or write them "by the seat of the pants." At some point you're going to have to formulate your copy, and if you do it early, it will keep you from writing a novel that is weak at the foundational level.

Adding a Tag Line

A memorable tag line can be an additional selling point. A tag line is a short, pithy encapsulation of the "feel" of the story. It's the sort of thing you find on movie posters.

One of the most famous tag lines was for the 1979 movie *Alien: In space no one can hear you scream.*

Perfect.

My suspense thriller *Don't Leave Me* is about two brothers, the younger of them autistic. When the older brother is targeted by bad guys, the younger brother gets drawn in.

My tag line: *When they came for him it was time to run. When they came for his brother it was time to fight.*

The tag line is used at the top of your cover copy. It's like the headline of an ad. Set it off by rendering the text in bold.

Here's what the sales page for *Don't Leave Me* looks like on Amazon:

When they came for him it was time to run. When they came for his brother it was time to fight.

Chuck Samson needs to heal. A former Navy chaplain who served with a Marine unit in Afghanistan, he's come home to take care of his adult, autistic brother, Stan. But the trauma of Chuck's capture and torture threatens to overtake him. Only the fifth graders he teaches give him reason to hope for the future.

But when an unseen enemy takes aim at Chuck, he finds himself running for his life. And from the cops, who think he's a murderer. A secret buried deep in Chuck's damaged soul may be the one thing that can save him. But can he unearth it?

Now, needing to protect his only brother from becoming collateral damage, Chuck Samson must face the dark fears embedded in his mind and find a way to save Stan … or die trying.

A Formula for Nonfiction

A simple formula for a nonfiction book description consists of three parts: a grabber headline, a section with bullet points, and a "Why should I listen to you?" paragraph.

Two types of headlines I advise you to choose from: the question headline and the promise headline.

The question headline, as you may have guessed, poses a

question that identifies a need, a desire, or a lack. The implication is that this book is going to fulfill that desire or need, or fix the lack. Two examples:

Do you freeze up and avoid people because it feels like they are judging and rejecting you? Is being self conscious preventing you from living your life?

(*Fearless Social Confidence* by Patrick King)

Are you deeply terrified of failure, rejection, and judgment? Does fear paralyze you and keep you from the life you want?

(*Fearless* by Zoe McKey)

The promise headline tells you the key benefit you're going to get from the book:

Discover the surprising secrets that will help you lose weight fast and keep it off—without dieting or exercise

(*Lose Weight Without Dieting or Working Out* by JJ Smith)

Skyrocket Your Productivity With This Simple, Proven Mind Hack!

(*Fast Focus* by Damon Zahariades)

You come up with great headlines like the old Madison Avenue copywriters did. You write a whole bunch of them, weed them out to a golden few, get feedback, and then choose the best one.

Next, you have a section with some lead-in text and a series of bullet points. This section needs to start with a sentence that has one goal, and one goal only: to get the reader to read the rest of the copy!

The legendary copywriter Joe Sugarman puts great stress on the first sentence. "Just remember that the sole purpose of all the elements of an ad is to get you to read the first sentence. Make that first sentence so easy to read that your reader is almost compelled to read it. If you grasp this, you've got an awfully good start and a great understanding of copywriting and the persuasive process."

For Michael Bamberger's book on the golden age of golf, the first line of the copy is:

Was golf better back in the day?

That perfectly encapsulates the premise of the book, a nostalgic look back at the era of Arnold Palmer and Jack Nicklaus and other legends of golf. It's short and sweet and does its job. It gets us to read the next paragraph:

> In *Men in Green*, Michael Bamberger, who fell for the game as a teenager in its wild Sansabelt-and-persimmon 1970s heyday, goes on a quest to find out. The result is a candid, nostalgic, intimate portrait of golf's greatest generation—then and now—that readers will cherish.

Now we get to the sizzle, the benefits. Set these off as bullet points. Your bullet points must sparkle. They must be concise and packed with promise.

One way to make sure you have that sizzle is by referring to this list of terms:

- How to
- Secret
- Key
- Critical
- Big
- Strategy
- Formula
- Mistake [to avoid]
- [A number, e.g., The 3 Big Secrets to...]
- What it takes to ...

Over the course of time, these terms have proven to be most effective. Thus, for my book *Self-Publishing Attack!* I used these bullet points:

- The single most important secret for ironclad profitability
- Step-by-step instructions for generating marketing copy
- How to think like a publisher so your e-books are discovered in a crowded marketplace
- Insider tips for writing books that sell, both fiction and nonfiction
- How to avoid the most common design mistakes
- The keys to an effective marketing campaign

Another way to get to the heart of your benefits is to use the phrase *You'll learn:* or *Learn how to:*

John Maxwell does this for his book, *Leadership 101:*

Learn how to:

- Follow your vision and bring others with you
- Produce a lasting legacy
- Grow the loyalty of your followers
- Make continual investments in the quality of your leadership
- Increase your ability to influence others
- Determine your leadership "lid"
- Empower others through mentoring
- Create a foundation of trust
- Use self-discipline to improve your character—and your results

An alternative to bullet points is to simply embed them in the description itself. I've done it both ways. Here is my copy for my book *The Mental Game of Writing:*

> In this book, #1 bestselling writing teacher James Scott Bell takes you through the mental landscape of the successful author. He shows you not only how to stay on your game, but how to improve it. He gives you insights, strategies and techniques for blasting through walls and jumping over hurdles, setting you free to concentrate on what you love most – writing.
>
> You'll learn how to define true success, formulate goals and plans, find courage and commitment to write, unleash your creativity and write with joy. You'll also be given steps to handle challenges like stress, burnout, envy, expectations and the trap of comparison.

Finally, you need to have a bit I call "Why am I listening

to you?" What authorizes you to write about this subject? How are you an expert? Do you have an advanced degree? Have you conducted studies?

Think of it as a short resume.

But what if you haven't got any of those things?

Then tell us what got you interested in the subject and what you've done about it (e.g., *John Smith has been a lifelong fan of the Detroit Tigers. He spent months in the baseball archives at the University of Michigan, poring over the writings of Detroit sports writers from the dead-ball era.*).

Find just the right tone that conveys your expertise.

Blurbs

There is really no way to tell if a blurb from a famous author significantly helps book sales. Common sense would say, as they did in the Lower East Side of New York in 1910, "It couldn't hoit."

So you can always ask.

But understand that the bigger the name, the more requests they get. They cannot possibly attend to every one. That's why so many of the A-listers have assistants to respond to requests with a nice rejection.

Don't hold it against an author if he or she can't offer you a blurb. Understand there are many reasons why this may be so.

I've seen some authors take favorable online reviews from consumers and quote them, with an attribution like this. "Great book! I couldn't put it down!" –Anne R.

Don't do it. It looks cheesy and is more of a turn off than an inducement to buy.

If blurbs mean a lot to you, then you need to network with writers who have something of a name. I cover how to do that in the chapter on networking.

Categories, Keywords, and Search Terms

The online bookstores allow you to categorize your books and put in appropriate key words to help searches. These help browsers find your books. They are important to have, but not obsess over.

A category is a broad umbrella for your type of book.

A keyword is a term that helps guide browsers to your books. That may seem confusing, because a keyword is not just a single word, but a term.

Kindle Direct Publishing (KDP), for example, allows an author to select two categories for a book and seven key words/terms to go along with those.

My novelette, *Force of Habit*, is categorized this way:

FICTION > Mystery & Detective > Women Sleuths
FICTION > Urban Life

My keywords are: *crime novels, Los Angeles fiction, nuns, martial arts fiction, noir, suspense, action thrillers.* Notice that some of these are more than one word. KDP gives you seven of these, separated by commas.

There are two terms that are very specific: *Los Angeles fiction* and *martial arts fiction.* If someone searches for those, the book will tend to be higher in the results.

The more general keywords, like *noir* and *suspense* are there to cast a wider swath, though that puts me in competition with many more titles.

Amazon has a few tips and rules for keywords you should know about:

Combine keywords in the most logical order. Customers will search for *military science fiction*, but probably not for *fiction science military.*

Use up to seven keywords or short phrases. Separate them

with commas, and keep an eye on the character limit in the text field.

Think about how you would search for your book if you were a customer, and ask others to suggest keywords they would use.

Useful keyword types

- Setting (Colonial America)
- Character types (single dad, veteran)
- Character roles (strong female lead)
- Plot themes (coming of age, forgiveness)
- Story tone (dystopian, feel-good)

Do NOT include the following in keywords

- Information covered elsewhere in your book's metadata—title, contributor(s), etc.
- Subjective claims about quality (e.g. "best")
- Statements that are only temporarily true ("new," "on sale," "available now")
- Information common to most items in the category ("book")
- Common misspellings
- Variants of spacing, punctuation, capitalization, and pluralization (both "80GB" and "80 GB," "computer" and "computers," etc.). The only exception is for words translated in more than one way, like "Mao Zedong" and "Mao Tse-tung," or "Hanukkah" and "Chanukah."
- Anything misrepresentative, such as the name of an author that is not associated with your book. This type of information can create a confusing customer experience, and Kindle Direct Publishing has a zero-tolerance

policy for metadata that is meant to advertise, promote, or mislead.

- Quotation marks in search terms: Single words work better than phrases—and specific words work better than general words. If you enter "complex suspenseful whodunit," only people who type all of those words will find your book. You'll get better results if you enter this: complex suspenseful whodunit. Customers can search on any of those words and find your book.
- Amazon program names, such as "Kindle Unlimited" or "KDP Select"

I suggest you begin by making a list of one-word descriptors. Try for at least ten.

Next, go to Amazon and then to the Books department. In the search box, type your first word and a space. What will happen is a list of the top search *phrases* will appear in order of popularity. Write these down. Do the same with your other words. Then go over your list and select a few of the terms that seem best to you.

You can also try Google's Keyword Planner. Go to YouTube and search for "Google Keyword" and you'll be directed to several tutorials on how to use this tool.

Your Author Bio

Simple rule: Keep it consistent with your genre. If you're a thriller writer, no need to go on and on about your flower garden.

Here are a couple of examples.

Scott Pratt is a successful indie author of legal thrillers. His bio is brief and direct, with a personal touch at the end.

Scott Pratt was born in South Haven,

Michigan, and grew up in Jonesborough, Tennessee. He is a veteran of the United States Air Force and earned a Bachelor of Arts degree in English from East Tennessee State University and a Doctor of Jurisprudence from the University of Tennessee. He lives in Johnson City, Tennessee, with his wife and four dogs.

In genres like romance and women's fiction, a more personal and relational bio is appropriate. Susan Meissner writes contemporary women's fiction with a spiritual touch. Notice that hers is written in the first person point-of-view, as if it were a note to a friend:

I cannot remember a time when I wasn't driven to write. I attribute this passion to a creative God and to parents who love books and more particularly to a dad who majored in English and passed on a passion for writing.

I was born in 1961 in San Diego, California, and am the second of three daughters. I spent my very average childhood in just two houses. I attended Point Loma College in San Diego, majoring in education, but I would have been smarter to major in English with a concentration in writing. The advice I give now to anyone wondering what to major in is follow your heart and choose a vocation you are already in love with.

I'm happy and humbled to say that I've had 17 books published in the last dozen years, including *The Shape of Mercy*, which was named one of the 100 Best Books in 2008 by Publishers Weekly, and the ECPA's Fiction Book of the Year, a Carol Award winner, and a RITA finalist. I teach at writers' conferences from time to time and I've a background in community journalism.

I'm also a pastor's wife and a mother of four young adults. When I'm not at work on a new novel, I write small group curriculum for my San Diego church.

Write out several author bios of different lengths and show them to people. Get feedback. Put your ego on hold. This is about attracting readers. Make them the focus of your bio.

Take a look at your bio from time to time. Give it a touch-up with any new and relevant information.

5

The Crucial Opening Pages

One of the great online boons to book lovers is the ability to view a sample of a book before purchasing it. On Amazon, users can download the first ten percent of a book for free or read it via the "Look Inside" feature. As an author, this gives you the opportunity to score a sale by making the reader want to read on.

On the other hand, with less leisure time these days, browsers are primed to find a way to say no to a purchase. Don't give it to them. As popular speaker Neil Pasricha wrote in *Harvard Business Review*, "I quit three or four books for every book I read to the end. I do the 'first five pages test' before I buy any book."

So what should these opening pages do? You've no doubt heard it expressed like this:

- Hook the reader.
- Grab the reader.
- Entice the reader.
- Get the reader to turn the page.

Nothing wrong with those terms, but the real question is: How do you make this happen?

Opening Pages of a Novel

Step 1: Create a disturbance

Use an opening disturbance in the first paragraph. A disturbance is anything that is different in the character's "ordinary world." This can be a portent, change, shift, challenge, trouble, danger, or another character.

A disturbance can be relatively quiet, or big and full of action. It can be an email or a monster. A doorbell or a gunshot. Tires squealing or a child crying. It can be virtually anything that causes a ripple in the character's life.

John le Carré, the great spy novelist, put it this way: "I think as a rough principle I always begin with one character and then perhaps two, and they seem to be in conflict with each other. The cat sat on the mat is not a story. The cat sat on the dog's mat is a story."

The opening disturbance works with any kind of book. Take a look at the following two openings. The first is a genre classic, the second a literary novel.

> They threw me off the hay truck about noon.
>
> – *The Postman Always Rings Twice* by James M. Cain

> Tina Antonelli stared at the heavy, cream-colored invitation like it was a loose diamond she'd unearthed in the sandbox at the neighborhood playground. No, it was even more valuable

than a diamond, she decided as she leaned against her kitchen counter and felt her night-gown-clad hip squish into something. Grape jelly, she thought absently, recalling her early-morning frenzy of sandwich making for school lunches. She reread the first line of calligraphy: Please join us in celebrating Dwight's 35th birth-day!

— *The Best of Us* by Sarah Pekkanen

Cain starts with a character in obvious physical distress. Pekkanen gives us something relatively quiet. But both are changes in the protagonist's ordinary world. Between those two poles are limitless possibilities for an opening disturbance.

Step 2: Put that disturbance in your opening line or paragraph

Dean Koontz used to have single-line openings packed with imminent trouble:

Penny Dawson woke and heard something moving furtively in the dark bedroom.

— *Darkfall*

Even before the events in the supermarket, Jim Ironheart should have known trouble was coming.

— *Cold Fire*

The "kicker" of the disturbance can be placed at the end of the opening paragraph, as Harlan Coben does in *Promise Me*:

The missing girl—there had been unceasing news reports, always flashing to that achingly ordinary school portrait of the vanished teen, you know the one, with the rainbow–swirl background, the girl's hair too straight, her smile too self–conscious, then a quick cut to the worried parents on the front lawn, microphones surrounding them, Mom silently tearful, Dad reading a statement with quivering lip—that girl, that missing girl, had just walked past Edna Skylar.

Step 3: Reveal the consequences of the disturbance

Now have your opening scene play out the consequences of this disturbance. As you do, be careful to avoid a backstory dump. Don't let too much explanatory material bog down the action. Sometimes a writer thinks the reader has to know everything about the background of a character before moving on, but they don't. Readers will wait a long time for exposition if they're intrigued by a character caught up in trouble.

A little bit of backstory is fine, but layer it in sparingly. Withhold as much as you can to create a mystery, another reason readers will want to see more—and click the buy button to get it.

When should you work on your opening disturbance?

The best time to work on your opening is after you've completed a draft of your novel. You know so much more about your story at that point that you can come back to the beginning and cut out what isn't needed.

A little trick that often works wonders is the "Chapter Two Switcheroo." Just toss out Chapter One and begin with Chapter Two. Usually you'll be amazed at how much faster your story begins, and how much information from Chapter One you can withhold until later.

Mickey Spillane, the famous hard-boiled novelist, once said, "The first page of a book sells that book. The last page sells your next book." Good, solid sampling will get your book sold. Then it's up to you to leave the reader wanting more.

Some Things to Avoid

Here are a few "no-nos" that some industry folks seem to mention a lot. While there are no rules here, certainly pay heed to these. If you decide to reject one, know exactly why you're doing so.

Excessive Description

"Slow writing with a lot of description will put me off very quickly," says agent Andrea Hurst. This is something you'll hear all the time from industry folks.

So how do you set an opening scene? Do it with an interplay of action and description. Get the action started first, then fill in just enough information to tell us where we are.

But you're a literary writer, you say. You love style. You live for the beautiful sentence. Well, if your prose is stunningly good, like Ken Kesey's opening pages in *Sometimes a Great Notion,* go for it. Just recognize that, by and large, literary fiction does not sell as well as commercial fiction. That may not concern you, but I need to mention that fact in a book on marketing.

Thus, you might consider the strategic decision to tweak your opening pages with the above suggestions in mind. Can you defer that wonderful, stylish description until later?

Have a look at this opening:

The day was sunny and breezy, if cool—
the first semi-decent weather after a long, hard,

bitter winter—and she didn't actually mind an excuse to get out in the world. She wouldn't take the cat, though; she would walk.

She stepped out the front door, shutting it extra hard behind her because it irked her that Bunny was sleeping so late. The ground cover along the front walk had a twiggy, littered look, and she made a mental note to spruce it up after she finished with the hellebores.

Swinging the lunch bag by its twist-tied neck, she passed the Mintzes' house and the Gordons' house—stately brick center-hall Colonials like the Battistas' own, although better maintained—and turned the corner. Mrs. Gordon was kneeling among her azalea bushes, spreading mulch around their roots.

This is actually a slight adaptation of a section from Chapter 1 of Anne Tyler's novel *Vinegar Girl*. But it's a later section, not the actual opening. It's heavy on description, not on action (which doesn't have to mean big action, just something happening with a bit of tension to it). I would like you to compare it to the actual opening:

Kate Battista was gardening out back when she heard the telephone ring in the kitchen. She straightened up and listened. Her sister was in the house, although she might not be awake yet. But then there was another ring, and two more after that, and when she finally heard her sister's voice it was only the announcement on the answering machine. "Hi-yee! It's us? We're not home, looks like? So leave a—"

By that time Kate was striding toward the back steps, tossing her hair off her shoulders with an exasperated "Tcch!" She wiped her hands on her jeans and yanked the screen door open. "Kate," her father was saying, "pick up." She lifted the receiver. "What," she said. "I forgot my lunch."

Which leads to a disturbing conversation.

My point is that for any genre, beginning with action and a disturbance is actually a marketing strategy, too, and is not a compromise of your artistic vision. You have a whole novel for that.

Point-of-View Fuzziness

"A pet peeve of mine is ragged, fuzzy point-of-view," writes Cricket Freeman.

This is especially important when writing in First Person POV. We need voice, we need attitude. Like Holden Caulfield in *The Catcher in the Rye* or Philip Marlowe in any of Chandler's books. Don't be bland.

I've read hundreds of opening pages by new writers over the years, and one of the most frequent mistakes is point-of-view fuzziness. It's a killer to intimate connection with character, which is key to grabbing a reader.

If you are a newer writer, and wish to make a strong run in fiction, let me advise you do some focused study on point-of-view. My book, *Revision & Self-Editing*, is one place to start.

Clichés

Agent Chip MacGregor has a list of opening clichés, including:

1. Squinting into the sunlight with a hangover in a crime novel.
2. A trite statement. ("Get with the program" or "Houston, we have a problem.")
3. Years later, Monica would look back and laugh ...
4. The [adjective] sun rose in the [adjective] [adjective] sky, shedding its [adjective] light across the [adjective] [adjective] land.

Other Pet Peeves

1. Descriptions making the characters seem too perfect.
2. Too much backstory.
3. Information dumps.
4. A grisly murder scene from the killer's POV.
5. Dreams.
6. Too much exposition in dialogue.
7. Whiny characters.
8. Characters who address the reader directly.

Opening Pages of Nonfiction

The Story Opening

Virtually any nonfiction work can open with a story or anecdote. Geoffrey C. Ward begins his massive, illustrated history of the West this way:

> Most of the men, women, and children of the Cocos Indian village on Galveston Island were away from their homes, setting traps for fish and gathering roots, one early November day in 1528, and so they did not see the pale,

half-naked man with hair on his face slip in among their huts. Moving warily, he stole an earthen cooking pot from one dwelling, grabbed fish from the rack on which they had been drying in the sun, tucked a squirming puppy under his arm. Then he fled toward the beach.

Three warriors did spot him and followed at a distance. When they reached the beach they were astonished to see nearly forty strangers much like the one they'd followed, huddled around a driftwood fire. Some were eagerly tearing at the half-dried fish, others were preparing to roast the stolen dog. Still others were simply sprawled on the beach, apparently too weak to move.

The Cocos were accustomed to trading with other native peoples living far inland, but not one of them had ever seen men like these before: most of them were pale and hairy, a few were dark skinned, all spoke a barbarous, incomprehensible tongue. The Indians hurried off for reinforcements. Soon, some one hundred warriors—tall men who pierced their ears and lower lips with reeds and were armed with bows and arrows—had gathered to see the curious newcomers.

One of the strangers tottered toward them, holding out a handful of beads ...

Kitty Kelly, a hugely popular (and controversial) biographer, knows how to grab your attention. Her book about the British royal family begins:

Princess Margaret strode out of the theater. She had barely managed to sit thorough the opening scenes of *Schindler's List*. She began squirming as soon as she saw the Jewish prayer candles burn down, leaving only wisps of smoke to evoke the ashes that would follow. She crinkled her nose at the sight of the captive Jewish jeweler being tossed a handful of human teeth to mine for filings. As the nightmare unfolded, she stiffened in her seat.

On screen, the streets filled with screaming Jewish prisoners, brutal Nazi soldiers, and snarling police dogs quickly emptied, except for the scattered suitcases of those Jews who had just been hauled off to the death camps. At that point the Princess bolted out of her seat.

"I'm leaving," she said. "I refuse to sit here another minute."

Her friends were aghast but immediately deferred to her displeasure. They left their seats and accompanied Her Royal Highness back to her servants in Kensington Palace.

"I don't want to hear another word about Jews or the Holocaust," said the Queen's sister. "Not one more word. I heard enough during the war. I never want to hear about it again. Ever."

Even a business book can start with story. Seth Godin's *Poke the Box*, a book about innovation, begins:

Annie Downs works at the Mocha Club, a nonprofit based in Nashville that raises money for the developing world by working with touring musicians.

Last year, she called her boss and said something she had never said before. "I've got an idea, and I'm going to start working on it tomorrow. It won't take a lot of time and it won't cost a lot of money, and I think it's going to work."

With those two sentences, Annie changed her life. And she changed the organization and the people it serves.

Now don't you want to read on to find out how? I do. And did.

The Solve-a-Problem Opening

This type of opening is good for how-to and self-help books. It hits you immediately with the problem you need to solve. It is effective in the same way mouthwash ads were in the 1950s. The advertisers first had to convince you that you had bad breath, that it would stunt your social life and maybe even get you fired. Then they offered you the solution!

Nothing at all wrong with that. It's a compelling way to draw readers in.

I've taught the craft of fiction for a long time. Over those years I've seen repeats of common blunders, the literary analogue of bad breath. So the opening page of my book, *27 Fiction Writing Blunders – And How Not To Make Them!* goes like this:

They see them all day long.

Agents and editors—whose job it is to find authors and manuscripts of promise—are used to spotting the most common errors of fiction writers. These mistakes, most of which are easily avoidable, spell probable doom for a project under consideration.

Readers see these errors, too. While most readers are not schooled in the craft of fiction, they nevertheless feel something is off. Their reading pleasure is dampened. If that happens too much, they are less likely to finish the book.

Or seek out another from the same writer.

Attention-Grabbing Statement

You can also start a nonfiction book by grabbing the reader by the lapels with a startling statement. This creates in the reader the expectation that you will be backing this up in the book, which is a good reason for them to buy it! (Of course, you need to ... back it up!)

Harvey McKay's book on street-smart career advice has a terrific title: *Beware the Naked Man Who Offers You His Shirt*. The opening lines:

> Could you or I have managed a major league baseball team to a World Series Championship?
>
> The answer is yes.

Quite a claim! McKay's book provides his evidence for making it.

Jay Conrad Levinson wrote a series of books with *Guerrilla* in the title. One of them is *Guerrilla Marketing Attack*. The opening paragraphs:

> You are surrounded. All around you are enemies vying for the same bounty. They're out to get your customers and your prospects, the good and honest people who ought to be buying what you're selling. These enemies are

disguised as owners of small and medium-sized businesses.

Several of the enemies are grossly larger than you. Some have the power and personality of Godzilla. Many of them are far better funded than you. Some have been successfully operating their businesses since prehistoric times.

Levinson's unspoken message is: if you don't want to get flattened by these powerful enemies, you'd better read my book!

So remember, first impressions—book cover > cover copy > opening pages. Make them irresistible, and you will have removed the barriers to the final action the browser takes: parting with his or her dough.

Which brings us to the issue of pricing as a marketing strategy.

6
What Price is Right?

Back when there was no e-book market to speak of (pre-2007), the pricing of books was left solely to the publishers and the bookstores.

A publisher set a price. Bookstores purchased books through a distributor at a discount. The bookstore could then decide whether to sell the books at the publisher's retail price, or offer an in-store discount to the consumers. Independent bookstores usually couldn't afford to do much of that, because the profit margin on print books has always been thin.

Then along came big chain stores like Barnes & Noble and Borders who could order more books at a better discount, and therefore were able to offer their customers even deeper cuts in prices (thus putting many smaller bookstores out of business).

Amazon grew into the one-stop shop to buy print books online, with even greater discounts and convenience (for example, virtually all books were "in stock").

Then, with the introduction of the Kindle e-reader in 2007, the e-book era exploded into reality.

And with it came all sorts of mayhem and madness in the boardrooms of the traditional publishing industry. Because consumers started saying, *Hey, why should we pay $25 for a hardcover when we can have it on a Kindle for under $10?*

This struck fear into the hearts of the (then) Big Six publishers, because they made most of their money off those hardcover margins.

Apple stepped into the mix when they introduced the iPad. Apple wanted to compete with Amazon for e-book dominance. So Steve Jobs started meeting with the big publishers, offering them "agency pricing" (meaning the publishers could set the sales price, unlike their deals with Amazon). In return, there was a tacit agreement to remove their books from the Amazon platform—unless Amazon also agreed to agency pricing.

A little group called the United States Department of Justice decided to take a look at what was going on. The DOJ did not like what it found. It took Apple and five of the Big Six to court on anti-trust charges. The DOJ won. Apple and the pubs appealed all the way to the United States Supreme Court. To no avail.

While all this was going on, a tsunami of self-publishing writers were putting books out via Kindle Direct Publishing and setting prices as low as 99¢. This put even more pressure on the Bigs, for now consumers were saying, *Hey, why should we pay $9.99 for an e-book thriller when we can get really good ones for $2.99 or $3.99 and even, gasp, 99¢?* There was no way a Biggie could match those price points and still keep their office space in Manhattan.

All that to say … price matters as a marketing tool!

If you are self-publishing and therefore in control of your pricing, here are your considerations:

Regular Price

What will be the regular price of your e-book? In order to collect the 70% royalty that Kindle Direct Publishing offers, the price of your e-book must be between $2.99 and $9.99. It should surprise absolutely no one who has ever a) taken an economics course, or b) gone shopping, that in general the higher the price, the fewer the sales. Of course, one makes more money off a higher price point. So it becomes a matter of trying to figure out what the "sweet spot" is for your particular book. What price will garner the most net income?

As of this writing, the conventional wisdom is that $2.99–$4.99 is the optimum range for fiction.

For nonfiction, a higher price point may be acceptable. According to Smashwords CEO Mark Coker, "Nonfiction buyers are less price sensitive. It appears as if most nonfiction authors are underpricing their works, and they should experiment with higher prices."

You should experiment with your pricing from time to time. I suggest a three-month window. For example, you might try an increase from $2.99 to $3.99 on a title. See how it goes for three months. Then assess whether or not to switch back.

Deal Pricing

You can change pricing temporarily to offer a "deal." Many authors do this by dropping a book to 99¢ and getting a boost from a deal-alert newsletter and social media outreach (I cover deal-alert newsletters in the chapter on "Things That Cost Money"). If you have books exclusively with Kindle, you can list your book for free for five days during each 90-day term in Kindle Select. I recommend using all five days in a row combined with deal-alert.

Perma-Free

Many authors who write series books like to price the first one permanently free on Amazon and other vendors. As of this writing, Amazon's Kindle Direct Publishing (KDP) does not allow a writer to use a free price point. To get a perma-free listing on Amazon requires a little workaround. You set your book free on *another* retailer, like Kobo or iBooks. Alternatively, you can seek distribution through an aggregator, such as Draft2Digital or Smashwords, which lets you set free as a price.

That's step one.

Step two is letting Amazon know that your book is free elsewhere. Go to your Kindle sales page on Amazon, and scroll to the bottom of the Product Details block. There you'll see "Would you like to tell us about a lower price?" Click on the link and you'll be prompted to enter a website URL and the information.

Sometimes Amazon is slow to respond to this. If it's not caught on in a few days, have a friend do the same report. If you have a KDP account, you can also contact them directly via the "Contact Us" link at the bottom of the dashboard, or via your Amazon Central account. Amazon is not against perma-free, so don't be shy.

Here is the all-important thing: be *sure* to put the links to the other books in the series in the back of your first book. Update those links each time you come out with a new book in the series. That way you'll make it easy for new fans to find the other titles.

Giveaways

Let me say something here about giveaways. These are campaigns to attract new readers by offering them a free copy of the book for a limited time, much like the free promo days offered by the Kindle Select program.

There has been a lot of chatter online about the overall value of giveaways. Jane Friedman (JaneFriedman.com/book-giveaways/) gives a balanced assessment:

> If there is a broader problem with give-aways specifically in the indie author community, it might be that you're possibly cultivating readers who don't give a damn about you and are only out for the cheapest read. In other words: giveaways can attract low-quality readers. But they attract high-quality readers, too. This is how business works. Some leads will be good. Other leads will be bad. Business savvy authors learn over time how and where to use the giveaway incentive to increase the high quality leads and reduce the low-quality leads.

Obviously, then, the use of giveaways requires time and business acumen to assess if you're finding those "high-quality leads."

Novelist Roz Morris, who has been into indie publishing for a long time, has this to say on her blog (January 25, 2015):

> Even giveaway campaigns to well-targeted readers don't seem to produce much return these days. I recently donated copies of *Nail Your Novel* for a fellow writer's launch campaign, which should in theory have resulted in more exposure for the series. I saw no increase in sales afterwards.

Bottom line: giveaways are not a crucial tool for your

success, especially when compared to what we've covered in the opening chapters of this book. The option is there for you if you find yourself itching to try something new. Just don't overestimate the ROI.

7

Productivity and Links

A writer writes, and doesn't stop until he's dead. Is that plain enough?

A true writer keeps going, no matter what. He continues to grow in the craft and the turning out of pages. As the late, great Robert B. Parker put it, "The most critical thing a writer does is produce."

But productivity is also a marketing tool. As prolific author Kristine Kathryn Rusch puts it, "The more you publish, the more readers will notice. Note that they will not buy everything or even anything, but they will recognize your name, which will put you in the conversation. In other words, it really and truly will help with discoverability."

The best way to be productive is with a writing quota. This was one of the earliest lessons I learned, and I've stuck with it my entire career. It has been, I believe, the single greatest factor in whatever success I've happened to achieve. Here's how to do it:

First, figure out how many words you can comfortably write in a six-day week. Maybe you can only squeeze in one hour of writing a day. In one hour you should be able to write a minimum of 250 words. Remember, a page a day (250 words) is a book a year!

That means in a six-day week you can comfortably write 1500 words. (Another great piece of advice I got was to take one day off from writing per week. For me that's usually Sunday. It recharges my batteries and gets me going fresh and eager on Monday. I commend this "writing Sabbath" to you.)

Now, up your total by 10%. You need to stretch a little. You need some pressure. If you can comfortably do 1500 words a week, make your weekly quota 1650.

Divide up your week into writing slots. Schedule them. Keep track of your daily and weekly output with a spreadsheet. On this spreadsheet you'll tally only the new words you write on a project you're aiming to publish. That means you're not allowed to do a Jack Torrance in *The Shining* and write *All work and no play makes Jack a dull boy* over and over.

You're accountable to yourself to keep producing. Get in that habit now.

As one successful hybrid (both self- and traditionally-published) author put it:

> Regardless of how you get your stuff out there, you have to keep doing it again, and doing it better. Most of us don't have the reliable income to quit our day jobs until we have four or five books out, with more on the way. You live off of your back list. And your back list remains viable because every time you release a new book, the old stuff gets a bump up. ("Fisking the HuffPo's Snooty Rant About Self-Publishing" by Larry Correia, December 30, 2016)

If you're a fiction writer, you can supplement your full-length work with short fiction. Publish the short fiction exclusively on Kindle and use their free promotion days to help readers find you. I have a chapter on that later on.

Links in the Back of Your E-books

Whether your publishing is self or tradish or a mix, you need links to your other books in the back of your e-books. Those links can go to a dedicated page on your website, or right to the retailer sales page. In the latter case, make sure that the links are retailer specific. In other words, your Kindle version should go to Amazon links. Your Kobo version to the Kobo pages (not Amazon), etc.

There are two things you need to know about linking to Amazon.

First, you are not allowed to use Amazon Associate links in your Kindle books. Being an Amazon Associate (also called being an affiliate) is a way to pick up some extra side money (if people use your affiliate link, you get a payment if they purchase that product, plus a slice of anything else they purchase on that particular visit). As an affiliate, you can use your account link on your website, in blog posts and on social media. However, Amazon Associate terms state: "It is not permitted to bookmark your links, send them in e-mails/newsletters, post in your Kindle books, or use them in any other offline manner."

Second, do not merely go to your book's Amazon page, copy the URL, and use that for the link. The reason is that there is all sorts of code in that URL that's specific to that particular visit. Instead, copy that URL and take off all the code that comes after the ASIN number. Thus, a URL to my novel, *Romeo's Rules,* might look like this:

https://www.amazon.com/Romeos-Rules-Mike-Romeo-Thriller-ebook/dp/B015OXVAQ0/ref=sr_1_1?s=digital-t e x t & i e = U T F 8 & q i d = 1 4 8 4 0 8 5 3 4 1 & s r = 1 1&keywords=romeo%27s+rules

A "pure" URL looks like this:

https://www.amazon.com/Romeos-Rules-Mike-Romeo-Thriller-ebook/dp/B015OXVAQ0/

I will use the above to create a bitly link. This allows me to track where clicks are coming from. If you want to take that step as well, got to bitly.com and follow the very simple process.

One further recommendation: make the first link at the back of your books one that allows your reader to sign up for your email list. When they've finished your book, and liked it (of course!) they are most primed to want to sign up. So make it easy for them. You might use language like this:

> Thanks for reading (Title). Please take a moment to sign up for my occasional email updates. You'll be the first to know about my book releases and special deals. My emails are short and I won't stuff your mailbox, and you can certainly unsubscribe at any time. Go HERE to sign up. And thanks again!

The care and nurture of an email list is another essential marketing tool, but one you need not stress over. That's the subject of our next chapter.

8

The Care and Feeding
of an Email List

There are two ways to grow a business.

The first is to go out and find new customers.

The second is to keep selling new products to satisfied customers.

For writers, the first way is all about *discoverability* and *conversion*. We have covered that previously.

The second is about *nurture* and *satisfaction*. Which is what the reader/fan email list is about.

You need to do three things:

1. Build up a list of readers who have opted to receive your emails.

2. Establish a regular routine of contact.

3. Give them something of value in every email (not what you're selling or linking to; what you're actually saying in your message).

Create an Account with an Email Service

First thing you need to do is set up an account with an email management service like MailChimp, Constant Contact, or Vertical Response. There are others, but these three get high marks. Once your account is live, you will filter all sign-ups for your email list through the service (which will provide you code for the form that you can use on your website). You include a sign-up link in the back of your books.

A word about pop-ups. When you land on a writer's blog or website, it's likely you'll be hit with a pop-up asking for your email address. This may come with an offer for a freebie the author is giving away. Pop-ups are controversial. Do they work? Or do they annoy just as many people as they attract?

Are the people who sign up for a freebie as valuable as those who sign up because they like something you've written?

I'm not going to try to settle the debate. As I write this, I am not using pop-ups because I personally find them annoying. Just one man's opinion. But certainly you can feel free to do your own research on the matter.

So let's talk about gathering those email addresses. The rule here is the same as we've established for all writers who hate marketing: *Do only those things that do not affect the quality of your writing, either through physical or emotional stress.*

If you have a website form and links in your books, that's enough. Because you want to focus on making "true fans," not just farming email addresses. The quality of your signups is directly related to their desire to follow you. Sending out emails to ten thousand people who barely know you is not nearly as effective as one thousand with whom you have a value relationship.

In an influential blog post titled "1,000 True Fans," Kevin Kelly says:

A thousand customers is a whole lot more feasible to aim for than a million fans. Millions of paying fans is not a realistic goal to shoot for, especially when you are starting out. But a thousand fans is doable. You might even be able to remember a thousand names. If you added one new true fan per day, it'd only take a few years to gain a thousand.

***

1,000 true fans is an alternative path to success other than stardom. Instead of trying to reach the narrow and unlikely peaks of platinum bestseller hits, blockbusters, and celebrity status, you can aim for direct connection with a thousand true fans. On your way, no matter how many fans you actually succeed in gaining, you'll be surrounded not by faddish infatuation, but by genuine and true appreciation. It's a much saner destiny to hope for. And you are much more likely to actually arrive there.

So how do you create a true fan?

First, you write great books. Remember, that's the single most important tool in all the marketing universe.

Second, you nurture the relationship with regular, value-added contact.

Let's discuss how to do that.

What Format?

The first decision you have to make is the format for your

emails. Should you use a newsletter-type of template? Or plain text, like an email to a friend?

This is not a throwaway question.

I don't use a newsletter look. To me it feels too much like advertising. That was my thought from the beginning, using only my personal preference as a guide.

But it turns out others are of the same opinion. Noted industry observer Jane Friedman has said we may have reached the point of newsletter fatigue because "the word is now out about the power of email marketing, it may feel like every journalist and author has a newsletter."

Popular blogger Anne R. Allen says, "Newsletters were big a decade ago, but there are just too many of them. And they're mostly self-serving and spammy."

There is data that backs this up.

In "Plain Text vs. HTML Emails: Which Is Better?" at Hubspot, the authors reported on a series of A/B tests, comparing HTML (and visual heavy) emails with plain text. The marketing industry was extolling the virtues of visuals. But the data showed that there was better deliverability and click throughs with plain text.

For example, shouldn't an email with an image of the e-book being promoted do better than an email with no visualization of the offer? Wouldn't just a plain email be boring, and not help explain the offer? Aren't humans wired to be attracted to beautiful design?

Unfortunately, this principle doesn't apply to email.

And the reason is simple: Email, unlike other marketing channels, is perceived as a 1-to-1 interaction.

Think about how you email colleagues and

friends: Do you usually add images or use well-designed templates? Probably not, and neither does your audience. They're used to using email to communicate in a personal way, so emails from companies that look more personal will resonate more.

They concluded:

It's not all bad though. Being limited to plain-text forces marketers to get creative with the basics—subject line, copy, positioning, link placement—to achieve the desired result. Sometimes "old-school," well-written copy is all you need to get the job done.

And just to add some anecdotal evidence, here are clips from two responses I got from one of my emails:

#1
Man, your emails are personable and as enjoyable as your novels! Congrats on releasing the upcoming Mike Romeo novels!

#2
I ALWAYS enjoy hearing from you … Talk about which, your email really cheered me up as 10 days ago I fell in our garage and injured myself!

Here is the email I sent that got those responses. I sent it November 29, 2016:

As December prepares to take the wheel

from November, and steer us toward the season of good cheer (Yes! We're going to have some good cheer even if it kills us!), I pause to ask a favor, with no obligation attached.

I am going to be releasing my third Mike Romeo thriller early next year. In anticipation of this, I would love to get some more reviews on Amazon for the first one, ROMEO'S RULES. Thus ... if you have read it and wouldn't mind leaving a review, even a line or two, I would appreciate it greatly.

And if you haven't read ROMEO'S RULES yet ... what are you waiting for???

I hereby declare that I am openly attempting to draw you into the series! To do that, I'm pricing the e-book at only 99¢ for the next couple of weeks. (And if I can tempt you to put it at the top of your "To Be Read" pile, and also have you review it, well ... consider yourself tempted!)

Here is the Amazon link:

[LINK]

What a crazy year it's been. I am so looking forward to Christmas with my family, in peace and quiet, watching *It's a Wonderful Life* (I hosted the first public showing of that film in many years, up at UCSB, when I was in film school. We got hold of Frank Capra himself and he brought a print up to the campus, and I got to be his driver ... that was so cool ...)

Anyway, it's been a good writing year for me, and I've got plans for keeping the keyboard hot throughout 2017. There's a fourth Mike Romeo in the works, some other fiction, and more books on writing. I can't thank you all enough for your support. It means the world to me.

So hoist some nog, do some shopping, watch some football, and snag as many See's caramel patties as you can. And when the fresh challenges of the New Year begin to present themselves, remember the sage advice of that great American philosopher, Yogi Berra: "When you come to a fork in the road, take it."

Pax,

Jim

Some Tips for Writing Your Emails

A big mistake budding authorpreneurs make is trying to sell before they've bonded.

What do I mean?

Simply this: consumers of anything don't want to be "hard sold." They want to trust who they are buying from.

The way you build trust is by doing things other than selling, things that get your audience to like you.

How do you do that?

By being the kind of person people like ... in your emails.

Use the "Guest at a Party" Rule

You're invited to a party at a private home. At this party will be many influential people and potential customers. You don't know anyone except the host.

How would you behave at such a party? Would you go up to the first person you saw and say, "Hi, would you please buy my book?"

No, you would be casual, friendly. You'd listen, and when

you spoke, it would be a pleasant bit of conversation. You'd try to say something that would interest the other person. You'd be genuine about this.

And that's the key: *genuine*.

Now, some say that when you "put on a mask" at a party you are not actually being "genuine." Not true. We all choose how to relate to people. There is nothing wrong, in a civil society, with being polite. (Of course, some also say we don't live in a civil society anymore. Okay then, do your part to reverse the trend!)

So in my emails I try to be what I'd be in a party situation. I want my readers to enjoy reading my emails. I keep them short. I don't waste time.

And because I've earned their trust, I can mention one action step. Rarely do I mention more than that.

Be Excited, But Not Giddy

Here's a clip from a sales e-letter I received:

> I'm so excited and can't wait to open the course tomorrow. I really want you to be a successful course creator. It really is addicting when you receive emails from your customers thanking you for the impact that YOU made on THEIR lives. You will come to understand that the impact you are making is more than making up for all the sacrifices you made to create the course.
>
> This is so exciting. I've known for a long time, that I needed to create this course and now that the finish line is so close, it kinda makes me wanna cry. Now, Now, there will be time for that later.

Emotion is good, but too much can taste sour. Here, the repeat of the words "excited/exciting" and "really" begin to feel manipulative, and "it kinda makes me wanna cry" is an overreach.

With that in mind, follow these steps:

1. Do a rough draft as passionately as possible. Pour yourself and your emotions into it. The above example would be good as a first draft.

2. Let it sit for a day.

3. Come back to it and tone it down 10%. How do you know how much 10% is? You just feel it, that's all. You'll know!

4. Cut overused words. Use a thesaurus to search for the simplest, most readable alternatives.

Here is how I would rewrite the above:

> I can't wait to open the course tomorrow!
>
> I really want you to be a successful course creator. It is addicting when you receive emails from your customers thanking you for the impact that YOU made on THEIR lives. You will understand that the impact you are making is worth all the sacrifices you made to create the course.
>
> I've known for a long time that I needed to create this course, and now the finish line is within reach.

One Call to Action

In my emails, I usually give one call to action. That means I want the readers to make one decision and use one click to get to the place where they can fulfill that decision.

Note, this is a different philosophy than the links in the back of your books. You can give multiple offerings there, because the reader who has finished your book, and likes it (of course!) can have a menu of choices. For example, if you're writing a series, you have links to the other books in that series.

Direct Link to Sales Page, Not Landing Page

Some writers use their email announcements to take their readers to a landing page, usually on their website. On that page the readers are then given further copy about a book and the various sales options. This is called a "two-step." Step one is clicking on the link in the email. Step two is clicking on the link that is provided on the landing page.

Studies have shown, however, that there is at least a 50% drop-off when someone is required to take an extra step. This, suffice to say, is deadly to sales.

Use one step instead. In your email, provide links that go directly to the sales site. For example, if your new book is coming out on multiple platforms, provide the links for those specific sales pages:

Amazon
Barnes & Noble
Kobo
iBooks
etc.

As mentioned earlier, Amazon Associates does not allow you to use affiliate links in emails. Follow the instructions I gave you for creating a "pure" URL and, if you like, a bitly link.

For other retailers (e.g., Barnes & Noble, Kobo, etc.) you can copy the URLs as given.

9

Your Website and Amazon Author Page

There are two primary pieces of internet real estate where you need to display your wares. The first is a website. The other is the page that Amazon gives you because you have books available in their store.

Website

Of course you need a website. Every business needs a website. And you, writer, are in business.

In no-stress marketing, your website is a landing place for people who are interested in finding out more about you. It doesn't have to be fancy. It doesn't have to be loaded with animation or pop-ups. It doesn't have to stress you out to create it or maintain it.

It just needs to be an easy-to-navigate, largely uncluttered place for people to quickly find out what you have to offer.

Register your domain. Use yourauthorname.com, if that's available. Otherwise, try yourauthorname.net.

Some authors with more common names might use: yourauthornamebooks.com.

You can hire someone to build a website. WordPress is a popular choice for the design, and there are many freelancers who specialize in it. Just beware: some of these folks can charge a lot of money for all sorts of bells and whistles you don't need. What do you need?

1. A clean design (i.e., not too busy, not too many elements on a page). You want to entice, not distract. I've seen home pages with all sorts of colors and different text fonts and random visuals, and I don't know what the heck to look at. You want people looking at your book covers (first impression, remember?) and some sales copy, and then links to the various places where the book can be bought (i.e., Amazon, Barnes & Noble, Kobo, iBooks, etc.)

2. An author photo. (Hint: don't let your son take a picture of you with his phone. Hire a pro. Look at author websites and find examples you like, and try to replicate that look. The author photo should be fairly close up so it shows in thumbnail or on a mobile screen.)

3. A short bio. More than five hundred words and you're starting to bore people.

4. A page for your books, or individual pages for each book/series. You'll have covers here, cover copy, and nice review blurbs (if any).

5. An email signup form.

6. A contact page.

At this point some authors are advised to add a blog. I do not offer that advice, because blogging is such a huge time-suck (I discuss that in a later chapter).

You'll want a website that's easy to tweak as each new book comes out. Feature your latest release on your home

Remember, readers are not interested in how fancy your website is. They want it to be clear and easy to get around in. They want to be able to find relevant information and not have to take a lot of time to get it.

Meet them more than halfway. Meet them *all* the way.

Amazon Author Page

Amazon provides each author selling on their platform a dedicated author page. Here you can upload your author photo, put in a bio, and show the covers of your books on Amazon.

You set up an Author Central account by going to: authorcentral.amazon.com

Then you can start customizing your page. The best way to learn what to do is watch a video. Go to YouTube and search for "Amazon author page" and you'll be presented with several tutorials.

Whenever you publish a new book, log into your account at Author Central and click on **Books** in the menu at the top. You'll be guided from there on how to add a new title.

As of this writing, you must set up separate Author Central accounts for the U.S. and the U.K. And, in fact, other international stores.

Start with the U.S. and U.K. and you can add others later as you desire. For U.K. go to: authorcentral.amazon.co.uk

This chapter is brief in order to give you the no-stress minimums you need. Any further activity that requires more time and effort than this begins to cut into your creativity and writing time, without elevating your sales to a significant degree.

10
Your Book Launch

S o you're ready to launch your book!

Congratulations! You and 175,341 other authors are going to be launching books at exactly the same time—and one of them is James Patterson!

But you have to do *something*. Let's make sure it's the right thing.

First, realize that a book "launch" is largely misnamed these days. Back when print publishing was the only game in town, a big company could launch a book (like a rocket, get it?) with huge promotion—e.g., big ads in the printed version of the *New York Times* and front-of-store displays in bookstores. Sometimes that worked; just as often, it didn't.

In the 1990s, for example, there were many over-advanced debut authors who didn't get enough altitude from a launch and ended up without careers because other publishing houses saw the lower-than-expected sales, and blamed it all on the authors.

Today, with so much competition for readers, a book launch really must be viewed more modestly. It basically comes down to getting the word out to people who already know you.

But some noteworthy authors see even that as a having limited reach. In an interview on Huffington Post (March 24, 2016), bestselling indie writer Hugh Howey states:

> I don't really [launch books]. Lately, I haven't even told readers that I had a new release. This isn't to be coy, or because I don't care, but because I haven't seen that it makes much of a difference. Maybe you can blow out the first week, but I've tried this every way possible, and I see the same general overall sales eventually. This won't be true for every author, but for me, the day after release, I'm writing the next story.

Good advice, that last part. Keep writing.

But I know you won't be able to sit back and do nothing. And I don't think you should (sit back). Instead, let's build a launch plan that is organic and relatively painless.

Start with the following:

Prepare a list of 10–20 people you know personally.

Prefab an email that explains your new venture, and invites the recipient to opt-in to your email list. Something along these lines:

> I just wanted to let you know that I'm about to become a published author. I spent most of last year finishing my debut novel, *The Adventures of Benjamin Disraeli in Space*, and it's going to soon see the light of day! It's a steampunk novel and was a lot of fun to write. Now all I have to do is get people to read it! I was hoping that you'd consider being one of those people, and maybe spread the word around when it's available.
>
> I'm going to offer it as an e-book first, for

99¢, to get the ball rolling. Would you consider signing up for my email list? That way you'll be the first to know when it's out. Here is the link to sign up: [LINK] Don't worry, I won't spam you or give out your email to anyone else!

You modify this prefab to fit each person on your list. For example, you can ask Uncle Henry how his auto body shop is doing, then put in the rest. You send these as personal emails, of course, not in bulk. (Your commercial emails must comply with CAN-SPAM regulations, which is what a reputable email service will walk you through.)

Even if you don't get all the folks to sign up for your email list, you've at least got the word out to many who know you that a book is coming out.

Some authors try to gather a particularly enthusiastic subset of their acquaintances to operate as a "street team." These are folks who agree to spread the word about your book when it goes live. You prepare for this by sending them a free copy (sometimes called an Advance Reader Copy, or ARC) a few weeks before publication date. When your book comes out send them a reminder email asking them to spread the word.

Note: Some authors ask family and friends to leave a review on Amazon. Amazon frowns upon this and has a way of analyzing IP addresses, etc. This can end up in reviews being removed and even a warning email from Amazon. Don't tempt them.

Reviews

Since we're talking about reviews, you will find services and strategies that purport to get you quality reviews. My feeling is that organic reviews are always best, and safest. There is dispute about how much sales punch reviews can deliver.

They don't affect your sales rank on Amazon. What they can do is provide potential buyers with some reassurance. But the only way to get good reviews is to write good books (our #1 rule). So don't stress about getting reviews. They will happen on their own.

Tom Combs is an indie writer whose debut novel, *Nerve Damage,* received a ton more reviews that most first efforts. I asked him what he did in this regard.

"Worked my ass off and wrote a kickass book (haha)."

Ah, there it is, our #1 tool again.

Tom continued, "I did mention to some in-person buyers that if they enjoyed the book, Amazon reviews helped me get it into more readers' hands. Shared that it was a challenge with the tremendous number of books out there. Otherwise nothing, though I received a decent number of emails from readers who loved it. To them I suggested sharing a review if they were inclined."

That is how you grow organic reviews.

Key Influencers

If there is someone you know who has a high "influence level" (i.e., a network in which he or she is a trusted voice), write a personal email offering the person a free copy, *no strings attached.* Tell this person that if they like the book, you'd appreciate a recommendation to the network.

For example, I know a writer who has a friend who became a big-time lawyer at a big-time firm. This lawyer friend likes to read thrillers. My friend wrote a thriller, gave the lawyer a copy, and the lawyer was happy to spread the news throughout his law firm. And no one got sued.

Blog Tours

On a blog tour, the author takes the first month or so of a book launch and tries to gain traction on blogs. That's not so easy to do anymore, with a gazillion blogs out there. Thus, a blog tour takes up a lot of your time, and usually does not result in significant sales. Keep that in mind.

You can try to arrange your own blog tour by reaching out to blogs on your own. You pitch your book to the blog administrator and offer to write a guest post, or be interviewed. The blogs you select might be those that are geared toward other writers (in which case you can talk about your writing method, or about the craft).

Or the blog might be one that deals with the subject matter of your book. If your thriller has some CSI razzle dazzle, a blog on forensics might be interested in your book.

There are outfits that will organize blog tours for you, for a fee. As with anything that costs money, *caveat scriptor*—let the writer beware. Check these companies out. Contact some of their past clients to see what they say.

And if you do go this route, learn the etiquette of blog touring. For example, you should be ready to interact with those who comment on your blog post when it appears. Be a good guest.

Avoiding the First-Book Blues

Ever since the self-publishing boom took off, authors and industry types have bemoaned the "discoverability problem." How can a new author, especially a self-publishing one, possibly get discovered in the tsunami of content flooding the market?

As Digital Book World put it back in 2014:

[D]iscoverability is becoming a bigger problem for authors and publishers. More books than ever are being published. Last year it was somewhere between half a million and a million new titles that were published in the United States alone. Self-publishing—mostly in the form of e-books without a corresponding print edition (digital first)—has greatly added to that abundance.

E-books have added to this overwhelming choice in another way, too. Books don't go "out of print" any longer. They now remain available as e-books basically forever. Thus the total catalog of books available to readers for purchase or download has swelled dramatically and may now be around the ten or twenty million mark (exact numbers are surprisingly difficult to come by).

A prominent agent (who also happens to be a friend) wrote about the problem. I want you to read the following quote carefully. There is one word that clonked me on the head and has led me to question the viability of that blasted buzzword *discoverability*. Here is the quote from her post "Solving the Discoverability Challenge":

Discoverability continues to be one of the biggest challenges authors face. The market is flooded with books; how are the people who would love your book ever going to find it?

The word that jumped out at me is *book*. Singular. That is a major clue as to how we've all been thinking about discoverability. And it seems to me that thinking's messed up.

Because it's based on an old-school paradigm. The traditional publishing industry does one book at a time for an author. This is called a frontlist title. They hope that title gets discovered. If they really believe in the book or the author, they'll put some money into advertising and bookstore displays. (In reality, that money now mostly goes to a new title by an A-list author.)

But in the new school of publishing, this paradigm has at least two major flaws.

First, readers hardly ever "discover" books. Rare indeed is it for a reader to float into a bookstore, spyglass in hand, scan the horizons, and suddenly spot a spine on a distant shelf, and then shout, "Book ho!" Still rarer for an Amazon browser who sees only a few of the gazillion thumbnails in the Kindle store.

The way readers find new authors is, and always has been, overwhelmingly (as discussed in Chapter 1) by word of mouth—through a friend, book group, a favorite reviewer.

Second, this view fails to emphasize that long-term writing success is not about a single book being found, but about an author building up trust with a growing number of readers.

So don't pin all your hopes and dreams on the launch of a single book. This is a career we're talking about. Keep writing.

But I will mention one more item to consider. Most debut authors who are self-publishing would benefit by going into Kindle Select and using the five free promotion days. No less an authority than Author Earnings' Hugh Howey agrees:

> I can also say without reservation that most debuting authors should go exclusive with Amazon until they gain traction and can afford to branch out. The increased visibility offered by Kindle Unlimited makes it worth thinking of Amazon as a writer's personal publisher. Keep in mind that self-published authors can move their works around. KU exclusivity is only for 90 days at a time. Unlike the decision

to go with a major publisher, where you lose all control of your work for the rest of your life—and another 70 years for your heirs' lives—with self-publishing, you can experiment freely. You can dip in and out and try lots of options.

In fact, you don't even need a full-length book to begin this process. Write a killer short story or novella and price it at 99¢. Then use the five days of free promotion, along with your social media, to get as many eyeballs on your work as possible. Think of this less as discovery than as the first step in establishing long-lasting trust.

Then make it easy for a happy reader to sign up for your email list.

11

Where We Are So Far

As a writer who mostly wants to write, so far you've been handed some good news about marketing. The best news is that the most important marketing tool is the one you already specialize in—your writing.

Three other items help to sell your books, and are passive. That means once you've set them in place, they remain to do their work without you. Which means you can get more writing done. They are, in order of importance:

- Your book cover
- Your cover copy
- Your opening pages

Next is price. You are looking for your fixed "sweet spot," as we discussed. That spot may change over time, so every now and again do a Google search for *self-publishing price "sweet spot."* You don't need any further effort on this point.

More good news: productivity counts. So do more of what

you love, write. Set up your system (quota-based) for consistent production.

We've covered growing an email list. Take the long-term view on this. Set up best practices to nurture your list, as we laid out in the previous chapter.

We talked about your website and Amazon author page, both of which, once they are in place, need only the occasional tweak.

Finally, we covered the launch of a book.

These are all things you can run with a minimum of stress, and out of which the greatest bulk of sales will flow.

By far.

Want to do more? That's up to you. In the chapters that remain, I'll explore some other moves you can make. I include them only for your perusal, and emphasize again that the marketing tools we've covered so far are the most important. So don't feel like you're missing out on some discoverability speed-boat if you don't do the things that follow!

You're cruising along nicely by writing excellent books.

12

Short Writing as a Marketing Tool

Write even more.

That's the subject of this chapter, specifically the use of short fiction to supplement your longer works.

Or short nonfiction as another way for readers to find you.

One strategy is to publish these short works exclusively on Amazon, via the Kindle Select program. This enables you to use five days of free promotion within a ninety-day period. You get the word out via your email list, social media (to the extent you use it), and influencers (those who have a wide platform who like your work).

So a fiction writer can get more fiction out there, and a nonfiction writer can explore subjects of interest. Your primary aim is to catch the eye of more readers and entice them (with your writing) to sign up for your email list. I recommend that at the end of your piece you offer an invitation to sign up and provide a link so they can do that. If your story or monograph relates to books you've written (e.g., you're writing a series and your story is about your series character), you can provide a link to the other books in your series.

And, after you produce several of these short offerings, you can put together a book-length collection and publish it at a higher price point.

In this way, nothing is wasted. You are writing, and making marketing headway with your writing.

Short Fiction

In my book, *How to Write Short Stories and Use Them to Further Your Writing Career,* I offer several reasons to write short fiction: to hone your craft, have fun, and to promote your other fiction.

It should go without saying that your story needs to be *good.* The nice thing is that you can get feedback on your stories fairly quickly. How? Beta readers. These are people you know and trust, who can offer you honest criticism and provide suggestions. You can hire a freelance editor, too. Writer's Digest offers the 2nd Draft service. Find that at WritersDigest.com under "Resources."

By submitting your work to be assessed by others, and taking to heart the notes you receive, you will be growing in your craft which, as we've seen, is part of the single most important marketing tool.

Monographs

A monograph is a short, nonfiction work that explores a single subject. In academic circles, these can run the length of novella in fiction, roughly 20K to 40K words.

But for our purposes, a monograph can be "Lincoln length." Somebody once asked Honest Abe, who was 6'4", just how long a man's legs should be. Abe said, "Long enough to reach the ground."

This applies to your monograph. Make it long enough to deal adequately with your subject, no more, no less.

In the early years of the self-publishing boom, I wanted to give writers instruction on how to set goals, how to manage time, and how to write comedy. I turned these subjects into monographs available on Amazon for 99¢ each.

13

Live Networking

Face-to-face (as opposed to digital) networking means connecting with other writers at a live event. This of course requires an investment of time and energy, but its occasional use has many things to commend it.

There are two basic kinds of conferences to consider: those that are primarily for readers, and those that are primarily for writers.

Reader conferences allow fans and writers to mix. Writers go to these conferences to hobnob and appear on a panel with a few other writers talking about their books. If you have published a novel, you can request to be part of a panel. But even if you're not on one, attending the conference at least gives you the opportunity to meet other writers and hear what's going on in the publishing world.

For example, writers of mysteries and thrillers extol the virtues of Bouchercon and International Thriller Writers, both annual events. Some of the big names in publishing show up and are usually open to casual conversation. The accepted wisdom is that the best such conversations are "at the bar" after the official day has ended.

Writing is a solitary endeavor, so getting some face time with other writers on occasion is a good thing. It's refreshing, and very often you'll pick up some tips about writing and publishing that can help you with your own practices.

Most cities have a writers group of some kind. The Mystery Writers of America, Sisters in Crime, and Romance Writers of America are a few of the national organizations that also have local chapters.

When you go to a conference, be sure to have business cards with your website and email address. Some writers bring bookmarks or postcard-sized ads for their books. Just be aware that those may get lost in a sea of other bookmarks and postcards. It's better to hand them out individually after a real conversation has occurred.

Don't go to a conference as a promoter. Go as a networker. Which means:

- Become the kind of person other people want to be around.
- Be brave enough to approach one or two people you admire, and who are doing things right. Ask for advice, but don't be a nuisance.
- Be a giver more than a taker. Providing someone with value, even if it's just a nice conversation, will gain you more than constantly asking for things.
- Politely remove yourself from toxic or negative people.

The other kind of conference you ought to consider is a reputable writers conference. This is where writers come to learn as well as to network with each other. It's a good use of your time because you're adding to your craft knowledge even as you connect with other writers, and, sometimes, agents and editors.

Do some research on conferences. You can find both national and local writers conferences online. Writer's Digest, for example, has a site devoted to writers conferences:

http://www.writersdigest.com/editor-blogs/guide-to-literary-agents/writers-conferences

When you find one that looks promising, go the website and check out the workshops and faculty. Look first for classes that address areas of the craft you need to improve.

Sometimes a conference will add an agent "pitch session" into the mix. This is basically speed dating with agents for five or ten or fifteen minutes, during which time you pitch your novel, hoping the agent will ask to have a look at your manuscript. This is one of the great stress inducers known to mankind. Thousands of writers each year rehearse and hone their "elevator pitches," and get tied up in Gordian knots as their time in the pitching room draws nigh.

Let me relieve you of such fears right now. You do not have to go through this torture. Prominent agent Wendy Lawton wrote the following on the blog of her agency, Books & Such, on January 16, 2017:

> More writers attend pitching workshops than ever before. They're honing their hooks and polishing their pitches. We're told that we need to be able to communicate our book to an agent in the time it takes to get from the first floor to the tenth floor in an elevator. It's sometimes even called the "elevator pitch" though it's more commonly delivered at a conference appointment with an agent.
>
> So do you suffer from pitching performance anxiety? Relax. Ditch the pitch. All is not lost if you can't wow the agent in 150 words or less. This pitch frenzy is born of a

publishing myth—that the best way to hook an agent is to pitch him. It's time to debunk that myth.

I'm not saying it's not important to be able to give a great summary of your book. It is. I'm saying that the traditional fifteen minute pitching sessions at conferences and the quick one-on-ones in elevators and hallways are highly overrated. So much pitch-tutoring has taken place in writing groups and at conferences that we hear nothing but stunning pitches these days—one after another. When every writer has perfect pitch, how does that help the agent? There's no doubt writers can pitch. The harder question is: Can they write? That can't be answered with a pitch.

The main thing to do, Lawton says, is right in line with the #1 marketing tool we've already discussed. "Write a stunning book," she says. "If your book is anything less than remarkable, don't expend the energy yet to connect with an agent. Put that time into the craft of writing."

Lawton also suggests that it's much better to personally engage with an agent—say, at a meal—and click on that level.

My advice to you in this regard is as follows: Don't be dull, and don't be desperate.

Have something of interest to say, and some stunning writing to show.

But don't stoop to cutesy or annoying ploys to get the attention of anyone. An agent friend of mine was once at a full table at a conference, chatting amiably with the writers, when another writer charged over, grabbed his arm, and knelt in front of him and said, "Please please please *please* represent me!"

It didn't work.

One other potential side benefit of a writers conference is that you might meet some folks who are at your same level who might be interested in forming an online critique group. Which brings me, ironically, to the subject of critique groups.

A good critique group can help you grow as a writer.

A bad one can hold you back.

The benefits of a small, dedicated group of writers are several. Novelist Jack Cavanaugh says, "Not until I joined a critique group did I begin writing for publication. The monthly meetings gave me a deadline, exposure to critique (which made me try harder to prove them wrong), and put me in contact with people who shared a common goal as well as information about publishers guidelines and needs. If it had not been for the critique group I may never have started writing seriously."

The experience wasn't the same for Robin Lee Hatcher. "I participated in a critique group around books 10 and 11. It was a horrid experience for me. I don't do well writing by committee, and since I am an intuitive writer, I work best without other input during the creative process. With rare exceptions, my editor is the first person who sees the book. Occasionally I will ask a trusted writer friend to read a scene or a chapter if I'm struggling with something, just to make sure I'm conveying what I hope to convey."

If you need that extra push, especially early in your career, then a critique group can help. But make sure the following factors apply:

- Look for people you have a rapport with. Previous relationships help.
- Keep the group small. Four to seven, give or take.
- Give as much as you get. Make sure you give adequate time to everyone else.
- Establish realistic deadlines and stick to them.

- Make sure the people in the group understand the genre you're writing in.
- Build trust. Check egos at the door.
- Be aware of the envy question. It happens. If someone's writing takes off, it may cause some strain. Best to talk about this up front.

14

Things That Suck Time

There's a concept in business called Return on Investment (ROI). It's often used in assessing what kind of marketing to employ. If I invest a certain amount of dollars, what can I expect in return?

When it comes to the writing life, I like to think of Return on Energy (ROE). You need to measure how you spend your time and effort. You especially need to ask if the energy you are expending on marketing and social media is having a negative effect on your creativity and writing output.

Large expenditure of time and energy in low-returning practices tire out your brain. Your imagination will want to take a hot shower and a nap. And the synapses that run your typing fingers will feel like an L.A. freeway at rush hour.

So beware of the things that suck your time. Here is my list of the suckers you have to be especially aware of.

Blogging

If you are a fiction writer and you think you might want to blog, let me give you a piece of advice: *Think again!*

Over the last ten years it seems that every man, woman, child, and cocker spaniel started a blog. The competition for blog traffic now is like the Russian peasants in 1905 seeking a side of beef. It's madness, sound, and fury.

And with increasing numbers of distractions—like apps and games and social media itself—fewer people are frequenting, or at least subscribing, to blogs.

But still there are agents and publishers pushing blogging as one of the ways an author can show that he or she is "serious" about marketing. They never, however, mention the negative ROE.

So if you think you want to start a blog, please first read "How to Blog: Essential Do's and Don'ts for Author-Bloggers" by Anne R. Allen. You can Google it.

Then, if you are a fiction writer, think it all through once more.

Nonfiction writers who have a special field of interest may consider blogging to be worth it. Why? Because you can create books from your blog material. You won't be "double-dipping" on your writing time. There's a terrific book on how to do this: *How to Blog a Book* by Nina Amir (Writer's Digest Books).

But there are alternatives to blogging on your own.

First, the group blog. If you can join with a group of other writers, at least one of whom is high energy and willing to administer the site, that would lessen the energy expended. It's still going to take a lot of time to establish a good presence on the internet.

The other way to go is to find one or two well-trafficked blogs and become an active member of the commenting community. Don't go there to hawk yourself, but to take part in real discussions. To offer value. To be a pleasing presence. Have a Gravatar (go to Gravatar.com for this). Your name in the comments should link to your website or Amazon author page. Also, if you've earned trust then you can, when the time comes, drop in a mention of your book.

Podcasting

Podcasting is audio blogging, and requires more time and effort than a written blog. Thus, it is best for nonfiction writers who have a tightly focused message and can produce enough content to keep an audience growing.

One way to do that is by interviewing other experts in the field.

If you love marketing and are dying to have your voice out there, have a look at the article "Podcasting and Indie Authors: Is Podcasting Right for You?" at *The Book Designer*, March 25, 2015).

But please understand that these two endeavors, blogging and podcasting, are *ongoing* time sucks. Once you're in, you're in for the long haul. And unless you become hugely popular, the effect on your sales is minimal.

There is also "video podcasting," which is like having your own little TV channel. But the cost in time, equipment, and effort to make it look good makes it something I cannot recommend to writers who hate marketing.

A less professional-looking—but perhaps for that reason more intimate—form of video casting is Facebook Live. The true value of this venue is for authors with a large number of fans who want to do some "nurturing" of that fan base. To do so requires preparation, strategy, on-air skill and so forth. Its value in increasing sales or making *new* fans has yet to be demonstrated.

Public Speaking

Nonfiction writers know the value of speaking to groups. They can target their audience by subject matter. After a talk on that subject, they can sell printed copies of their books "at the back of the room." A good speaker can make hundreds, if not thousands of extra dollars that way.

Fiction writers, especially those just starting out, have a much tougher road. They may be able to get invited to a local library or community college classroom. They will probably find themselves speaking to four or five people. The amount of E in the ROE is large: time and travel. The R in the ROE is usually quite small, even with book sales in the back of the room.

Many authors don't care about—or are frightened of—public speaking. Heck, many people fear public speaking more than they fear death.

So don't worry if you're not out there speaking in public. It's not going to make a huge difference in your overall marketing.

If you do speak, however, do one thing. Begin each talk by taking out a yellow legal pad (or something like it) and announcing that if anyone would be interested in getting updates on your book deals, please write down *legibly* an email address. These people are consenting to be put on your email list.

When the talk is over, as soon as you can put the emails into your email database, segment it (e.g., "Library talk, January 2017"). Then craft a short, personal email to those folks:

a. thanking them for coming to your talk.

b. telling them you won't be spamming them.

c. saying you're looking forward to letting them know about future books.

d. giving them a tone that is friendly and even a little humorous.

e. thanking them again, and signing off.

Interviews

With some research you can find podcasts and blogs that do regular interviews with writers of your profile. What you need to do is assess the reach of these venues.

For example, it's not good ROE to invest an hour giving an interview which may reach only one hundred people. That's because the expected sales result from such appearances is usually less than 1%. So out of one hundred listeners, one will buy your book. That will bring you around $2.00 on a book priced at $2.99. Was an hour of research, an hour of prep, and an hour of talk worth the price of one tall coffee at Starbucks?

It's easier to answer some written questions for a blog. Do some research first, and look for a blog that generates lots of comments.

Book Signings

When traditional publishing and brick-and-mortar bookstores were the name of the game, all authors tried to arrange book signings. A big-name author, like Stephen King or Dean Koontz, had this handled by their publisher or PR firm. A dozen big bookstores all over the country (or region) would advertise the appearances, stock a freighter-load of copies of the new book, and wait for the lines to form.

Which they would.

But for midlist authors, the road was not quite so smooth. Usually, they would have to do the legwork with local bookstores to try to set something up. If they did get a gig, they'd show up at the store, which provided them with a folding table and a chair, and try to generate some interest from browsers who kept walking by, looking at them with suspicion or pity. Usually it was your best friend, and perhaps your mother, who ended up buying copies.

And that was in the good old days!

Today, with physical bookstores shuttering, signings by authors are drying up. Browsing for books is increasingly done online. When people go to a Barnes & Noble or local independent store, they usually have an exact idea of what they want.

And it is not your book.

If you want to sign books at a store, apply the ROE principle. Know that you will spend a lot of time for very little return. Is it worth it to you? Or could you be putting your time to better use elsewhere?

One exception to this is the book launch party. You arrange for a store to stock your book, and invite as many friends and fans as you can to join you at the store. You have refreshments, give a little talk, read a little from your book, maybe answer some questions.

It's fun. When I launched my Ty Buchanan legal thriller series with the hardcover release of *Try Dying,* I arranged to have a signing at one of the great bookstores in Los Angeles, The Mystery Bookstore (no longer there, unfortunately—another casualty of commerce). I knew the managers there and had supported the store. So they gave me a signing, and I put out the word to my family, friends, and business associates. My wife planned the refreshments. And we packed the place.

A good time was had by all. And I sold a lot of books.

But this was a party. A one-time event. As part of an ongoing marketing plan, I have not done a bookstore signing since 2012.

15

Things That Cost Money

Sometimes you just want to do something, anything, to get the word out. Even if it costs you money.

That's why advertising was invented.

It's also true that advertising rarely makes you a profit. If it's a good ad in a good place, you might break even or make a little scratch. But you really need to think of it as an investment, paying to gather readers who will become fans who will, in turn, buy your books. That's where you make the profit, in ongoing sales.

Deal-Alert Newsletters

There are a number of sites that have subscribers who have agreed to receive a daily alert about e-book deals. Authors pay for placement in these alerts and arrange to have their books priced below what they normally charge. Thus, a book that is normally priced at $3.99 might be on special for $0.99 or free for the day the alert comes out.

The Big Kahuna of these newsletters is BookBub. With a

subscriber base in the millions, BookBub reaches more potential readers in all the popular genres than any other such service. Thus, landing a placement with BookBub is highly competitive. Their turndown rate is over 80%. It can be frustrating, because BookBub doesn't offer specific reasons for a rejection. All you can do is keep trying. According to BookBub, the main factors they consider are:

1. The discounted price. Is it at least 50% less than normal?

2. Overall quality of presentation (i.e., cover, no typos, etc.).

3. Number of "authentic" reviews. While BookBub doesn't state a minimum, odds are better the more reviews you have.

4. "Accolades" from trusted review sources, or well-known authors.

Don't despair if (actually, *when*) BookBub turns you down. There are other newsletters. Remember, you shouldn't mind if you end up spending a little money to make new readers.

Some of the better-known deal-alert newsletters:

BookGorilla
Kindle Nation Daily
The Fussy Librarian
eBookSoda

Online Advertising

In my experience, paying for an online advertisement is not a good investment. There have been tales of those who have done well with, say, Facebook ads. But there are also tales of woe in this regard. My evidence here is all anecdotal, so certainly conduct your own research if you wish to try these waters.

BookBub now offers paid advertising spots. As does Amazon via Kindle Direct Publishing. These two, it seems to me, would be the best venues for your advertising dollars. Learn what makes a good ad and experiment. I've done a few ads with both BookBub and Amazon. I designed these ads using Canva.com.

My experience tracks closely with that of writer Eliot Peper, reporting on the Reedsy blog (March 12, 2016):

> Across all 10 [Amazon ad] campaigns, I ended up spending almost $10 for every $1 of incremental sales. Marketing enthusiasts might point out that the $1 doesn't take into account customer lifetime value because readers might very well decide to buy more of my books later. While true, I don't have rigorous enough analytical tools to eliminate that effect from the data. Regardless, I'm quite confident that the discrepancy wouldn't come close to materially impacting the results.

Paid advertising is an expensive add-on to any marketing campaign. It also takes time to design, test, and assess ad campaigns. For writers who would rather be writing, it's not necessary.

Experiment if you like, just don't stress about it.

Book Trailers

At one time book trailers were the hot new toy for authors. They have cooled off considerably.

The problem is that in these times of slick movie and TV

and game trailers, done on budgets beyond authors' pocket-books, it's hard to compete on a quality level.

Many of the early book trailers were little more than slide shows with some music, and a bit of text. Some prominent authors tried their hand at "movie-style" trailers, complete with actors. These usually look like amateur film student projects.

And most of these trailers were too long. Thirty to forty-five seconds is the correct range, in my opinion.

But the effect on books sales is negligible at best.

16
Platform Paranoia

A platform! My kingdom for a platform!
– Richard III, after his novel was rejected by a publisher.

Ah, platform. Why do I loathe thy name?

Because it is constantly pushed in the faces of writers, luring them away from the most important thing they do, which is write.

And because, if you're trying to get a book published by one of the Bigs, they will tell you a platform is somehow "essential" to your success these days. Only they won't tell you how big a platform is supposed to be, nor exactly how to create a platform. They may not even know how to define a platform except via vague generalities like "how many people you reach."

And if you're a new writer, you're liable to fall into platform paranoia. This is manifested by you looking at every other author's platform and trembling because they are everywhere ... and you're not!

The Definition of Platform

The word platform comes from the old world of public

speaking. It is the place where a speaker stands to address a crowd. The Lincoln-Douglas debates were held on platforms.

In the internet age the word has come to be equated with the number of "followers" a person has online. These followers are supposed to be people who know about you, engage with you, like having you around. Thus, if you put the word out on something you've written, they are to be magically transformed from followers into buyers.

It's that last bit that's the kicker. For these days you can acquire a boatload of followers. There are companies who will get them for you (for a fee). Or you can follow fifty thousand random people on Twitter and get forty thousand following you back.

You can build the numbers. But what you really need to build is trust. And that takes time. Lots of time. And effort.

The Real Deal About Platform

A well-regarded agent, Janet Grant, blogged at her Books & Such Literary Agency site (January 16, 2017) about what an agent is looking for in a client. She said, in part:

> Today publishers want authors who are heard and seen. The author needs to be prepared to make a big marketing fuss when her title is released. That's now an inherent part of a writer's life.
>
> I'm looking for clients who get that and have applied themselves to building an e-mail list of readers, a plan for promoting their books, and a significant Internet presence.

The prompted a comment from me:

> Janet, how does this apply to a new writer of fiction? How is that writer supposed to build an email list of readers without readers? I think this causes undue and unwarranted stress for a writer who should be 95% focused on one thing: the writing, making it the best it can be. Because only that kind of writing inspires readers to become fans who sign up for an email list in the first place.
>
> I also worry about "platform paranoia" over what constitutes a "significant internet presence." What's this new writer supposed to do? Be on FB, Twitter, Pinterest, Instagram, YouTwitFace, and blog? When we all know now that social media does NOT sell books in any significant way … and that being spread over too many places (and especially blogging) is time-sucking quicksand away from the writing that actually matters.
>
> Now, I can see why publishers worried about dwindling revenue want to lessen their risk. That's simple business sense. But this kind of blanket "requirement" placed on the shoulders of new authors is not the way to go about it, IMO.
>
> Besides, if a new or emerging writer does manage to have boffo social media and a strong email list, and if that author is being asked to shoulder most of the marketing anyway, shouldn't that author also be asking why he or she is only getting 17% of the pie?

Janet responded, in part:

> But fortunately most publishers have come to realize that a new fiction writer doesn't have the ability to do so. That means what the person is writing is receiving a publisher's attention rather than having a built-in platform.

Wendy Lawton, Vice President of Books & Such, remarked in February of 2017, "I've sold 15 books so far [this year] and I'd have to say that the majority of those, including one very impressive multi-book program, came from authors with no platform but a compelling idea. For fiction, platform is much less important ..."

Which means you need not suffer any paranoia about platform.

You can keep the main thing—your writing—the main thing

17

Social Media Madness

In 2007 the lovers were born. Soon they met and conceived a bastard child. The child looked so beautiful ... until ... Damien!

What's this? A riff on *The Omen*?

Nay, for it really happened. The lovers were the Kindle and Twitter. And their child is that brain-eating spawn, social media marketing.

When the child turned one, writers were just starting to figure out they could profitably self-publish on the Kindle platform.

They also saw Twitter exploding with users. They began to reason: Hey! What an easy way to reach a zillion potential book buyers! All I have to do is tweet out, "My new thriller is not to be missed. Buy it here!" and keep on tweeting that same message. Over and over. A dozen times a day. The money will pour in!

Which it never did, of course. For authors and businesses soon woke up to the harsh reality that Twitter is not great shakes at direct marketing. In fact, it is barely any shakes at all. It is social, and personal ... but it is no citadel of commerce.

Still, addicted to hope, authors jumped upon each shiny new social media outlet that appeared. Pinterest! Instagram! Tumblr! Google+!

This addiction was fueled by enablers. Writers hoping to catch the eye of a traditional publishing house were being advised by agents and editors and critique-group chatterboxes that a gigantic social media platform was an absolute necessity for success!

Biggest load of flapdoodle since Fen-Phen, with just as many ruinous side effects.

Here's the truth: social media madness is eating your brain, affecting your ability to concentrate and work deeply, and sabotaging the quality of your fiction—which is the one thing you cannot afford to have sabotaged if you want a long-term career!

Social media stimuli is actually akin to a drug addiction. Really. Brain scans show that constant internet users have similar brain patterns as drug addicts and alcoholics. And since social media involves another "you," the social-you, the branded-you, the you you want to present to the world, there's a dopamine effect. You get a good jolt of pleasure when you post, because it's easy and it's all about you. Which in turn makes you crave more of it.

The book *Deep Work* by Dr. Cal Newport is an eye-opener on all this. The gist of the book comes from its cover copy:

> Deep work is the ability to focus without distraction on a cognitively demanding task. It's a skill that allows you to quickly master complicated information and produce better results in less time. Deep work will make you better at what you do and provide the sense of true ful-

fillment that comes from craftsmanship. In short, deep work is like a super power in our increasingly competitive twenty-first century economy. And yet, most people have lost the ability to go deep—spending their days instead in a frantic blur of e-mail and social media, not even realizing there's a better way.

A prominent agent described social media correctly as "an ongoing conversation that an author has with an audience." Which audience? Your audience, however many that happens to be. When you have conversations, you are not doing the hard sell. Nor should you.

A *Publishers Weekly* column (November 18, 2016) said the following:

> As social media platforms evolve, adding new tools, mobile offerings, and enhanced personalization, indie authors are evolving with them. Facebook, Twitter, and the other major platforms are more crowded than ever, requiring authors to find more creative ways to be heard above the noise. Compounding this challenge is that these platforms have been adjusting their algorithms to filter posts for perceived relevance. (For example, this summer Instagram introduced a new way of ordering posts "so you'll see the moments you care about first," as the company described it in a statement.) This results in promotional messages being pushed lower on users' feeds or filtered out altogether, putting added pressure on authors who are seeking ways to attract followers and gain attention.

One way around this is for authors to put greater effort into tailoring their social media messaging. "It's important for authors to interact in an organic way—don't set up your Facebook page and just say, 'buy my book,'" says Carol Palomba, social media manager for the author submission service Writer's Relief and its Self-Publishing Relief and Web Design Relief divisions. She has taken to advising the indie authors she consults with to avoid promotional language in their posts and, instead, to "talk about yourself, where you're getting inspiration from, and share what would be of interest to readers and followers."

Narrow Your Social Media Presence

On the site *Digital Book World* (December 16, 2017) Chris Syme stated:

> There are hundreds of social media networking sites on the Internet. Of those, there are 10 or so that most people can identify. According to data from Smart Insight, there are around 2.3 billion people on social media worldwide.
>
> Five years ago, it was pretty easy to be found and followed on social media. Now, the Internet is bulging with information. And this proliferation of bits and bytes has caused some authors to throw up their arms and declare that selling books on social media is not possible.
>
> Today, learning how to sell more books with social media involves pulling back, not

widening out. If you narrow your focus instead of casting a wide net, you can concentrate on engaging on one channel and being present for conversations without the huge time commitment (and stress) of going wide.

The secret to selling more books with social media is designating one primary channel to engage with your readers and developing the rest as outposts where you set up a redirect to your primary channel for readers who find you there. If readers know you are connecting with fans online, they'll make one more click to find your primary channel.

Syme also had an amusing breakdown of what the more prominent social media outlets were like if one were to take the perspective of a wine connoisseur (*Digital Book World*, March 7, 2016):

> To make good decisions about where to invest your marketing resources (time, money, skills), you should know a thing or two about channel culture. No two channels are the same. Each one is like a small civilization with its own unwritten rules of interaction and behavior....
>
> *Facebook: I like wine*
>
> *Twitter: I am drinking #wine now*
>
> *YouTube: Here is my video on how to choose wine*
>
> *Instagram: Here are pictures of me drinking wine*

LinkedIn: Hire me. I am a wine expert

Pinterest: My collection of all things wine

One might add *Goodreads: The gang's all here, drinking lots of wine, and sometimes things get out of hand!*

Here is my advice regarding social media.

Pick *one* platform to specialize in.

One.

Pick the one you enjoy most, or think you can handle best.

If you want to have a presence on other platforms, to experiment, go ahead. But place your focus on one.

Use it to the extent you enjoy it, and no more.

Use it for actual engagement with those who follow you.

Be a good content provider, and a good listener.

Avoid venting your spleen on social media. Because besides being a lousy place to sell books, it's a horrible place to take controversial positions. There is no true discussion here, because that's not what social media is set up for.

Don't post drunk.

Make all people glad they follow you.

Earn trust. When it's time to mention a book, you'll have earned the right to do so.

Tame Your Social Media Madness

Writing a quality novel is hard work. So the moment you get to a challenging spot, your brain starts to crave the easy pleasure and fast distraction of hopping onto the internet. The more you follow that impulse, the stronger the impulse center grows.

Thus, you'll be distracted from your writing all the time. Your ability to concentrate and stay engaged, and actually work through a writing problem toward a breakthrough, will weaken. You'll be like a former champion pole vaulter who has started to take frequent breaks from training to snag donuts and coffee. Instead of vaulting to greater heights, the bar is going to have to be set lower and lower. Pretty soon, you'll be doing The Limbo.

After reading Newport's book, I saw how much of it applied to me. I'd fallen into bad habits. Too often as I wrote I'd find an excuse to go check social media, which took me out of "flow" and often kept me distracted far too long.

So here's what I've done:

1. I do not do any internet surfing or social media that I do not schedule beforehand.

2. When I write, I write. I set a timer to my writing in bursts of about 34–40 minutes. I take a short break, then write in another spurt. During this time I do not hop on the internet (except when I have to do some on-the-spot research for part of a book. But usually I try to save my research time for another chunk of my day). I do not answer my phone, unless it's a family member.

3. Before a writing spurt, I'll write down, on paper, my times for the internet, email, etc. Then I'll stick to that schedule.

Bonus tip:

To get more writing done, I am usually working on 2–4 fiction projects at a time, and something nonfiction. Usually that means I have one fiction project on my front burner, another on my back burner, and one that I am editing. In addition, I have a few that are "in development" as a movie studio might say. I also have some nonfiction projects at various stages.

Isaac Asimov was one of the most prolific authors of all time. He wrote science fiction and nonfiction books on various topics that interested him, from the Bible to Shakespeare to Math. In his autobiography *It's Been a Good Life* he writes:

I don't stare at blank sheets of paper. I don't spend days and nights cudgeling a head that is empty of ideas. Instead, I simply leave the novel and go on to any of the dozen other projects that are on tap. I write an editorial, or an essay, or a short story, or work on one of my nonfiction books. By the time I've grown tired of these things, my mind has been able to do its proper work and fill up again. I return to my novel and find myself able to write easily once more.

Don't let social media madness devour the good parts of your creativity and your production as an author. Tame it. If you have to, shame it. But always schedule it, and stick to the program.

18

If You Want to Go Further

So there you have it—marketing for authors who hate marketing.

Yes, we must all do *some* marketing. But the things we do can be chosen wisely and performed without stress. If, however, we fall for the idea that we have to do it all, and that someday a magic wire will be tripped, with us sitting in the catapult, and that will send us soaring into the rarified air of the highly successful writer, well, there lies madness and diminishing returns.

For all of it pales to what we've said is the most important thing: writing books that people want to read. Writing them with a craft that keeps getting better.

Do that, and you will begin to grow a readership.

Don't do that, and all the fancy marketing in the world is not going to make you lasting fans.

Think about everything not in terms of marketability, but "trustability."

Will your readers trust you?

Will they trust that when they spend precious time and a

couple of bucks on a book you wrote, that you will benefit them in some way?

Will they trust that if they sign up for your email list, or follow you on social media (the *one* you've chosen to specialize in), that you will provide them quality content and even some interaction when warranted? That you won't pepper them with "buy my book" messages?

That's what creates the long tail, the continuous sale of books to both new and satisfied readers.

When you launch a book, you put some energy in the right places.

When you want to fish for more readers, you can spend some money on a deal-alert newsletter.

But the most important thing you will do is get to work on your next book.

In fact, you will become a prolific writer, because writing is your business and your calling, your meat and your motivation.

Now, if you find yourself wanting to go further, to try some new things, by all means go ahead and do some research. Just understand that nothing you add to the mix will be more important than your books themselves ... ever. So don't let any form of marketing anxiety creep into your creative consciousness!

Two places where you can begin to do some further research:

TheCreativePenn.com, hosted by Joanna Penn. Joanna has written a book on marketing, but also has abundant material via her podcasts (transcripts provided) with ideas about marketing.

KrisWrites.com, home of fiction writer and business author Kristine Kathryn Rusch. Under "Business Resources" on her website look for "Discoverability Series."

Writing Resources

Finally, here are a few resources for you to continue your writing journey.

First, please take a moment to sign up for my occasional email updates. You'll be the first to know about my book releases and special deals. My emails are short and I won't stuff your mailbox, and you can certainly unsubscribe at any time. If you do sign up, I'll put your name in the random drawing I do each month for a free book.

You can sign up by going to:

www.jamesscottbell.com

There's a box for your signup in the sidebar.

Online Course

Writing a Novel They Can't Put Down

A comprehensive training course in the craft of bestselling fiction. An investment that will pay off for your entire career.

The books below are by me unless otherwise indicated:

Plot & Structure

Write Your Novel From the Middle
Plot & Structure
Super Structure
Conflict & Suspense

Revision
Revision & Self-Editing
27 Fiction Writing Blunders - And How Not to Make Them
Self-Editing for Fiction Writers (Renni Browne and Dave King)

Dialogue
How to Write Dazzling Dialogue

Style
Voice: The Secret Power of Great Writing
Description (Monica Wood)

Publishing & Career
How to Make a Living as a Writer
The Art of War for Writers
How to Write Short Stories and Use Them to Further Your Writing Career
Self-Publishing Attack!

Writing & the Writing Life
Just Write: Creating Unforgettable Fiction and a Rewarding Writing Life
Kindle Edition
The Mental Game of Writing
Writing Fiction for All You're Worth
Fiction Attack!
How to Achieve Your Goals and Dreams
How to Manage the Time of Your Life

Nonfiction
On Writing Well (William Zinsser)
Damn! Why Didn't I Write That? (Marc McCutcheon)

Recommended Writing Blogs

KillZoneblog.com
WriterUnboxed.com
WritersHelpingWriters.net
HelpingWritersBecomeAuthors.com
TheCreativePenn.com

CPSIA information can be obtained
at www.ICGtesting.com
Printed in the USA
FSHW020954020621